TONY BLAIR

ABOUT THE AUTHOR

Steve Richards became political editor of the *New Statesman* in 1996, a year before Tony Blair was elected as Prime Minister. He was also a columnist for *The Independent* and presenter of ITV's live political programme, *The Sunday Programme*, for most of the New Labour era. He interviewed Tony Blair several times and also had many private conversations with him when he was Labour leader and Prime Minister. His books include *Whatever It Takes: The Real Story of Gordon Brown and New Labour*, *The Prime Ministers* and *Turning Points: Crisis and Change in Modern Britain, from 1945 to Truss*.

TONY
BLAIR

STEVE RICHARDS

Swift

SWIFT PRESS

First published in Great Britain by Swift Press 2025

1 3 5 7 9 8 6 4 2

Copyright © Steve Richards 2025

The right of Steve Richards to be identified as the Author of this Work has
been asserted in accordance with the Copyright, Designs and Patents Act 1988

Typesetting and text design by Tetragon, London
Printed and bound in Great Britain by CPI Group (UK) Ltd, Croydon CRO 4YY

A CIP catalogue record for this book is available from the British Library

We make every effort to make sure our products are safe for the purpose
for which they are intended. Our authorised representative in the EU
for product safety is Easy Access System Europe, Mustamäe tee 50,
10621 Tallinn, Estonia gpsr.requests@easproject.com

ISBN: 9781800754409
eISBN: 9781800754416

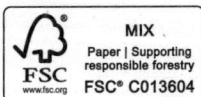

CONTENTS

INTRODUCTION

T ONY Blair was easy to misread as leader and Prime
Minister. In spite of intense scrutiny from the moment
he acquired the leadership of the Labour Party, nothing
was quite what it seemed. Blair was seen widely, not
least by himself, as a bold radical. In reality, he was often
extremely cautious. Over Iraq and some other policy areas
he was viewed as messianic when he was being characteristically expedient. He made many calculations in relation to
Iraq, but one was to cling to the apparently safe orthodoxy
in which the UK stands 'shoulder to shoulder' with the
United States in war. Only Harold Wilson challenged that
conventional view, over Vietnam. Oddly, Wilson is seen
as a greyer and more deviously pragmatic leader than the
seemingly crusading Blair. More widely, many saw Blair
as a liar, to the point of criminality. This was simplistic.
He took seriously the notion of integrity in public life. He
tried in many different ways to form a relationship of trust
with the electorate.

Wherever an observer turns there are contradictions. Blair is perceived as a 'moderniser' and yet he sought to strengthen the traditional institutions that partly define the UK, from the monarchy to the military. To Margaret Thatcher's public appreciation he partly cemented her legacy rather than move on from it as far as privatisation and the significance of the private sector were concerned. At the same time, he was a change-maker. The UK in 2007 was a different country to the one it had been in 1997. The changes were not as great as those introduced by Clem Attlee after 1945 or Margaret Thatcher after 1979, but they were of historic significance. From devolution, which played its part in establishing peace in Northern Ireland, to civil partnerships and a revived NHS, Blair left Britain in a better place than it had been. He was also a different type of Prime Minister, partly a consequence of his youth. On his first weekend in Chequers he was photographed wearing a denim shirt, not the Prime Ministerial gear associated with John Major or Ted Heath. He could be both casual and conventional.

Increasingly, Blair sought change by rising above his party. Here was another curious contradiction. He could be appealingly self-deprecating in speeches and interviews, but quite soon his rule became personal, almost presidential – a leader in spite of his party. He proclaimed, often with an apolitical verve, that what mattered was not whether a leader was on the right or left but whether he made the 'right decision'. 'It was the right thing to do,' he explained in relation to a variety of contentious measures. In doing so he was inadvertently challenging the essence of democratic politics, in which parties debate with intensity what is 'right' and why.

Was he a visionary, impatiently looking ahead, or a leader trapped by his past: Labour's vote-losing 1980s and the dominance of Margaret Thatcher? He was both. Constantly fascinated by politics, he sought always to focus on future challenges, while his vision of what might follow was limited by his narrow interpretation of what had happened to Labour and of the rise of Thatcher in the decades that preceded his elevation to the top.

The Labour Party has struggled to make sense of him, in the same way that the Conservatives are still trying to work out the significance of Margaret Thatcher and whether she should continue to be their model long after she ruled. Was Labour's move to the right under Blair necessary in order for the party to win, or could they, after 18 years of Tory rule, have afforded to be more daring, more left-wing, than their leader wished to recognise? Keir Starmer, another landslide election winner from opposition, wrestles with the question. Partly he follows Blair, but on some policy issues he is closer to a traditional Labour leader.

In order to pin down the elusive Blair we need to start on the day he became Labour leader. He opened with an inspiring speech of energetic focus that was also shaped by caution. The self-constrained visionary was beginning to take shape.

CHAPTER 1

Leader

WHEN Tony Blair won Labour's leadership contest during the hot summer of 1994 he became both a youthful leader of his party and the likely next Prime Minister. Most Leaders of the Opposition have to work hard in order to be perceived as the next occupant of Number 10. Some never manage to acquire the flattering aura that tends to feed on itself. In Blair's case the perception was fully formed from the moment he became leader.

This was not all his doing. The Conservative government was in disarray, torn apart over the issue of Europe and still bewildered by its act of regicide in the autumn of 1990, when Margaret Thatcher was forced from power. Labour was well ahead in the polls before the leadership contest had become necessary. Yet surveys also showed that Blair was unusually popular with the wider electorate.

He had a boyish charisma that managed to inspire and reassure simultaneously. He was highly focused, seeming to know where he wanted to take his party and the country, while being humorous and modest. On the sunny morning of 21 July 1994, at the age of 41, the newly crowned leader appeared to be a winner on many levels: in command of his party and with high personal ratings in the country, alongside a media rhapsodising about his attributes. Most Labour leaders rarely experience such a potentially intoxicating brew even in their honeymoon phase. Conditioned to losing elections, Blair was smart enough not to become intoxicated, at least in the early years of his leadership.

His triumphant coronation took place against a background of contradictory forces, impressions and developments. Beyond the seemingly glowing surface there were complex ambiguities. On one level, the circumstances of Blair's extraordinary rise could not have been more propitious. Like Harold Wilson in 1963, he won the leadership mid-term, filling a vacancy that arose from the sudden death of a leader. Hugh Gaitskell's death had paved the way for Wilson. John Smith's death necessitated the contest that Blair had won. Gaitskell and Smith had both seemed to be in place for the long haul. As a result, their successors arrived with a rare streak of dutiful purity. They were filling a gap that had arisen unexpectedly and not as a result of endless scheming. Wilson had been the only Labour leader to win an overall majority from opposition, and had evidently benefited from acquiring the role when mid-term disillusionment with the ruling Conservatives was deep.* That was also the case with Blair in 1994. Only Keir Starmer has won as Labour Leader of the Opposition after having served a full term in that role. Oddly, Starmer was helped in his ultimately triumphant marathon by his obscurity during the period of the Covid pandemic, when he was rarely seen in public. He became prominent as a leader around mid-term, so not very different from Blair and Wilson in terms of exposure as a Leader of the Opposition.

Blair's victory was further proof that, after four successive election defeats, Labour's membership was opting for steely pragmatism. During John Smith's leadership Blair increasingly stood out as a 'moderniser' who, along with his close colleague Gordon Brown, had looked for inspiration from President Clinton's victory in the United States. Clinton won the election in 1992, the same year that Labour had lost yet again. In 1993, Blair and Brown flew to the United States to spend time with senior Democrats, seeking to find out more about how Clinton had won and what the lessons were for their party. Their visit caused considerable internal tensions at Westminster. The moody shadow cabinet member John Prescott referred to Blair and Brown dismissively as 'the beautiful people' while they were away. He was not alone in wondering what they

---

* Clement Attlee is often cited as the first victor from opposition, but he had been Deputy Prime Minister in the wartime coalition more or less up to when the election was called.

were up to. As a new Labour leader, Smith handled such tensions with considerable skill. Self-confident enough not to worry about the motives or ambitions of colleagues, he gave Blair and Brown space to pursue their 'modernising' ideas and also allowed the likes of Prescott to fume. Smith's self-confidence was much missed when he died, even if some followers of Blair and Brown saw this rare quality in a Labour leader as complacency. He gave colleagues room to breathe. Quite a few of them breathed noisily, but he did not feel threatened as they did so.

In this context Blair was becoming increasingly prominent. Under Smith he was Shadow Home Secretary and had acquired distinctive definition with the sound bite 'Tough on crime, tough on the causes of crime', a slogan that no previous Labour leader would have disagreed with and yet one that Blair managed to make fresh, not least in the view of the mighty Conservative-supporting newspapers. Brown was its author, but it was Blair who benefited from the juxtaposition in the perception of colleagues and the media.

His approach as Shadow Home Secretary was part of a pattern. As Shadow Employment Secretary under Neil Kinnock's leadership, Blair had campaigned to reverse the party's support for the 'closed shop', in which employees were compelled to join a trade union. He continued to speak to journalists working for Rupert Murdoch's newspapers when the Labour leadership had instructed MPs not to do so in the 1980s. Blair was the most articulate campaigner for changing the way Labour elected its leader, a highly charged issue during the Smith era. The party did revise the rules at its conference in 1993, and Blair became the first leader elected under a partial version of what was known as 'one member, one vote', in which the block vote of unions was replaced with individual union members casting direct votes, alongside MPs and party members, each group comprising a third of the total. He was constantly challenging perceived orthodoxies within his party.

In slightly different ways, Blair, Brown and Peter Mandelson, who had been Labour's media guru in the 1980s, were seeking ways to widen the party's appeal by reforming its internal procedures and revising policies. Of the three, Blair's background was the most unusual for a potential leader. As he described it himself in a speech in April 1995, 'I wasn't born into this party... I chose it.' His father had been a Conservative. Blair had attended Fettes, a grand private school in Edinburgh, Scotland's equivalent to Eton. At Oxford University he was not politically active. It was only afterwards, in the mid 1970s, when he met Cherie, his future wife, and senior Labour-supporting lawyers, including Derry Irvine – who became a cabinet minister in Blair's first government – that he become fascinated by the party and addicted to politics. While active in Hackney in north London, he had the outsider's capacity to analyse how the party at national and local level might be seen by those who were not part of the various internal battles in that stormy decade in which a Labour government often ruled precariously, with no majority. As he recalled in his memoir, while he searched intensely for a seat in the build-up to the 1983 election – he had been willing to move from London to the north-east in the hope of securing one – he 'took care not to depart too far from the party mainstream opinion at that time, much to the left of where it had been; but I was nevertheless aware from the beginning that we were in the wrong place'.

At Oxford, Blair was detached from party politics, attracted to the ideas of a charismatic Australian Anglican vicar, Peter Thomson, who spoke inspiringly on ideas around Christian socialism and communitarianism, but largely disconnected from the debates raging around the Labour Party. The art of performance, an important part of his later political personality, was learned playing in rock bands rather than at the Oxford Union.

Perhaps there was always one echo from his Oxford days. Blair's overt pragmatism was always layered with a tonal evangelism. Even before he became an MP in 1983, he was fascinated by the power of language in politics, the potency of the well-framed argument. In his memoir he describes hearing the former cabinet minister Tony Benn speak on behalf of Cherie, who was standing in Thanet North, a safe Conservative seat, in the 1983 election. Benn was then the most prominent figure on the left of the party and had been for more than a decade. He was a spellbinding orator, as Blair remembered: 'I sat enraptured, absolutely captivated and inspired... What impressed me was not so much the content – actually I didn't agree with a lot of it – but the power of it, the ability to use words to move people, not simply to persuade but to propel.' This is an astute analysis of Benn's skills as a speaker. As Blair suggests, even then his politics were different from those of the Labour left, but by the time he became leader he deployed the power of words more effectively than any other British politician of the time. Like Benn he could cast a spell over a room, each word carefully chosen, employing humour as a political weapon to bind speaker and audience even more closely. There was a melodious quality to Blair's delivery, as there was to Benn's. The difference was that Benn sought to put the case for sweeping, radical change, whereas Blair's mesmeric exhortations hailed small, incremental reforms, an accommodation with the long period of Tory rule rather than a huge leap away from it. In a way, Blair's speaking skills were even more impressive than Benn's. He made the cautious seem exciting.

In his opening speech as leader he was at the start of a journey, a term he later used as the title of his memoir. He cited the word 'socialist' or 'socialism' several times and rooted himself on the 'left of centre'. Soon these terms were no longer to feature as part of the Blairite lexicon. Before long he claimed to be at 'the radical centre', a term that manages to sound exciting and reassuring while lacking precision. The references to socialism rarely got a look-in.

They did so in his first speech as leader, delivered at the University of London's Logan Hall on 21 July 1994, but couched firmly in a context in which Blair was already navigating what became known as 'the third way':

> We need neither the politics of the old left nor new right but a new left-of-centre agenda for the future, one that breaks new ground, that does not put one set of dogmas in place of another, that offers genuine hope of a new politics to take us into a new millennium. I said then that socialism was not some fixed economic theory defined for one time but a set of values and principles definable for all time.

The juxtaposition between old and new was in place from day one of Blair's leadership. Soon this was to become a clever and more precise assertion. He was leader of 'New' Labour. The past was 'old'. The new divide was not left versus right as much as a chronological one. He was moving on, choosing neither old left nor new right but a politically safer path:

> On the economy, we replace the choice between the crude free market and the command economy with a new partnership between government and industry, workers and managers, not to abolish the market, but to make it dynamic and work in the public interest, so that it provides opportunities for all. On education, that we do

provide choice and demand standards from the teachers and schools, but run our education system so that all children get that choice and those standards, not just the privileged few. On welfare, that we do not want people living in dependency on state handouts, but will create a modern welfare system that has people at work not on benefit.

The speech conveyed a sense of purpose and confidence that Blair had noted in Benn's address in Thanet. Here was a framing of an argument after which the policies would make more sense.

Blair's confidence was partly based on a deep knowledge of the Labour Party's capacity to lose elections. Elected in 1983 when Labour was slaughtered, he had seen firsthand how the party had repeatedly been defeated. Indeed, he endured an earlier experience of Labour's unpopularity, having contested the Beaconsfield by-election in 1982, shortly after the Falklands War. Blair noted then how many voters in the safe Conservative seat saw Thatcher as a great Churchillian leader following her victory in that conflict, not least compared with a Labour leadership regarded as 'soft on defence'.

Sharing an office with Gordon Brown, also elected for the first time in 1983, he observed closely the leadership style of Neil Kinnock, whose epic attempts to change Labour only resulted in failure in 1987 and 1992. In particular, the 1992 election had a decisive impact on Blair.

Shortly before the vote, Kinnock had been snubbed by President Reagan on a visit to Washington, while Thatcher was treated like a revered equal when she made trips to the White House. At the start of the election campaign the then Shadow Chancellor, John Smith, had unveiled a shadow budget that included some increases in income tax for higher earners. The Tories and the media leaped on the proposals and they became 'Labour's tax bombshell'. The reason Blair was ready to lead in 1994, when the vacancy had arisen so suddenly and unexpectedly, was that he, Brown and Mandelson, by then an MP, had talked constantly for years about what Labour leaders were doing wrong and what in their view was necessary to put it right.

Both Blair and Brown were drawn to Mandelson with a near-unqualified admiration, and he reciprocated, identifying the duo as the party's most telegenic communicators, with a clear sense of the need for Labour to change. Mandelson's impact shines much light on Labour's relations with modern media before and after his arrival. He had been a producer on ITV's *Weekend World*, a weekly current-affairs programme, and therefore understood how TV worked. For this reason alone he was treated with reverence by those parts of the Labour Party deeply concerned about its chronic inability to project through the media to the wider electorate. It shows how far the party had fallen behind the times in terms of modern communication that the arrival of a single producer from a TV programme with a relatively small audience triggered such waves of excitement from the likes of Blair and wariness from those irrationally suspicious of the techniques required to communicate effectively.

By the time of Smith's death, Blair had a clear sense of how he wished to position his party and about some of the policy implications that arose from that positioning. His ideas were not based on deep reading of some of the party's more favoured philosophers, from Karl Marx to R. H. Tawney, the latter a favourite of Neil Kinnock and his deputy, Roy Hattersley. Blair was not one to cite Anthony Crosland, author of the influential *The Future of Socialism* (1956). But he had become a world expert on Labour in the 1970s and 1980s and why the party lost elections.

In standing for the leadership and planning for what would follow, Blair had already acquired a steely focus arising from his expertise. But preparing for government was a different matter. Blair had never been a minister. He had never been inside Number 10. Brown, too, had no experience of power. Mandelson had only been an MP since 1992. At least Smith had experience of government, as had his deputy Margaret Beckett, who had been a minister in the 1970s. Even Blair's newly elected deputy, John Prescott, had never been in government. In every other respect, however, Prescott could not have been more different from Blair. The party's new deputy had risen through the union movement and had almost made an art form out of being inarticulate. His sometimes incomprehensible sentences acquired a sense of their own. Prescott could be irascible and insecure but, if he felt part of a project, was passionately loyal. He also had a fascination with policy detail, albeit erratic and indiscriminate, that at times went deeper than some of those in the New Labour project.

Blair managed Prescott deftly. The two remained leader and deputy until Blair's resignation in 2007, despite the fact that quite a few in the media had assumed the dynamic would not be sustainable for very long. The far more fundamental partnership, though, was between Blair and Brown: it was one based on seething and complex tension, while also being a relationship that defined New Labour and gave it durability.

From 1983, Blair had been the junior partner. Brown arrived at Westminster immersed in the history of the party, having largely flourished in a Scottish Labour Party well known for its capacity for internecine warfare. Brown also knew a bit about the media. He had briefly been a BBC producer in Glasgow, and was also a voracious reader of newspapers as well as books. He was gripped by politics, regarding his vocation as a moral mission, though it was one that was accompanied by a deeply competitive streak and intense personal ambition. In the late 1980s, Brown stood in as Shadow Chancellor when Smith suffered a heart attack and more than held his own against the formidable and ideologically self-confident Chancellor, Nigel Lawson. For a period, Brown almost dared to assume that at some point he would be Labour leader. Many in his party and the media shared the assumption in the late 1980s, including Blair. But, from the election defeat of 1992, Blair was becoming more of a dazzling star, the subject of flattering profiles in newspapers and magazines, increasingly prominent in the media. Meanwhile, Brown was now Shadow Chancellor and beginning the long haul back to a position where Labour could be trusted to run the economy. In the early years that involved preventing colleagues uttering a word that implied a spending commitment. In doing so, his internal popularity took a hit. He had no idea there was going to be a sudden leadership vacancy as he played the role of the iron Shadow Chancellor. No one did.

Even so, when Smith died Brown was taken aback to discover that an unstoppable bandwagon for Blair was hurtling towards the leadership. Evidently, Blair was going to stand. Brown was traumatised. A close friend had died suddenly. Another close friend was intent on claiming the crown. Brown considered standing and convinced himself he could win by attacking Blair from the left. But he knew that in doing so he would be placed by the media as a figure on a part of the political spectrum it largely loathed. His deep ambition and the embryonic project that the duo had been working on would implode. Probably there was a part of him that knew he would lose. Blair had momentum, but it took an act of uneasy ruthlessness for the younger of the duo to make the move. As Blair told Roy Hattersley, the party's former deputy leader, before he formally declared, 'Gordon wants it more than me.'

Brown did and was determined to establish a power base as a condition of his support. Famously, the two met at Granita, a restaurant in Islington, to reach some form of agreement about what Brown could expect if he did not stand and also endorsed Blair. There had been other, preliminary meetings, too. The duo had spent so much time together, and now suddenly they were meeting in an unrecognisably changed context. Since 1983, they had been nearly always united in the various internal battles that marked Labour's long route back to power. Now they were battling it out between themselves. Brown left convinced that Blair had agreed to step aside for him at some point in a second term of government, and that he would have free rein over policies relating vaguely to social justice. Blair took a different view in relation to the commitment to stand aside.

Whatever was formally or informally agreed was less relevant than the explosive assumptions made by Brown that he would exercise considerable power as Chancellor and succeed Blair in a second term. The apparent imprecision of the arrangement and the conflicting interpretations of the two participants were the source of tension from the beginning, fuelled by ideological differences that were underestimated then and have been since. Blair knew from day one, in July 1994, that he had a formidable rival breathing down his neck.

As ever with the New Labour era, the tensions were nuanced. On one level the early manifestations were a warning of what was to come. Suddenly the media started to refer to 'Blairites' and 'Brownites', terms that had not been used before the leadership contest. Early attempts at definition were imprecise, although there were substantial differences between the two sides when they moved into government. Most immediately, Brown hardly acknowledged Mandelson. Brown had a loyal team. Blair had his own. Yet there was also formidable collaboration. Brown helped to write Blair's opening speech as leader, the earliest possible sign that they could still cooperate powerfully. They had discussed so often how Labour should change that there was no way the discussion could stop now that the junior member of the partnership had become leader.

Blair was both pragmatic and evangelical, in a strong position while facing an intimidating and complex rival – the contradictions were deep and persistent. There was one additional significant conflict in the early years of Blair's leadership: he proclaimed he was leading his party, and ultimately the country, on a new political journey, while his immediate policy agenda was acquired largely from the past. Blair was formed by the old and the new. By the summer of 1994, John Smith had proposed a minimum wage, expressed support for the 'Social Chapter' that was part of the European Union's Maastricht Treaty, established the Commission on Social Justice, agreed to a referendum on electoral reform and made several internal reforms, including a new method for electing a Labour leader, passed at his final party conference in 1993. All of these policy areas were central to New Labour's pitch. This is in stark contrast to the challenge faced by Keir Starmer when he sought to be another Labour leader to win from opposition in 2024 with the claim that he had changed the party and was ready to do the same with the country. Starmer scrapped the entire 2019 party manifesto and began the daunting task of policy development with a blank sheet of paper. His policy programme was far less developed than that of Blair, who had inherited much from Kinnock and Smith.

Yet Blair managed to convey a sense of a fresh start. He did so partly on the basis of his own personality. He was much younger than Smith and sought a dynamic and ruthless team to drive his project forward. On becoming leader, Blair was determined to woo Alastair Campbell as his press secretary, having failed to convince the political editor of the *Sunday Times*, Andrew Grice, to join him. Blair was the first Labour leader since Harold Wilson to be fascinated by the media and its importance in delivering any message to the wider electorate. In this respect, the contrast with Smith was marked. Smith was uninterested in how the media worked. On one evening during his leadership, he was scheduled to deliver a speech. He read what he was going to say that morning in *The Times* newspaper. Baffled, he asked his press secretary, David Hill, why *The Times* was reporting a speech before he had spoken the words. Hill explained that papers rarely report a speech after it had happened, so he had briefed them in advance.

Smith's indifference to the fickle media was a virtue in some respects, but problematic for an opposition party that had a unique capacity to lose elections via hostile newspapers that influenced the broadcasters.

From the moment Campbell accepted the post he worked tirelessly to secure positive coverage. This tirelessness became part of the media fascination with Blair. The newspapers had slaughtered Michael Foot and Neil Kinnock. They were lukewarm about John Smith. Suddenly, relations with a Labour leader were more complicated for normally Tory-supporting newspapers. Already they had turned on John Major. Editors were missing what they saw as the bold strength of Margaret Thatcher. They wanted another strong leader. Blair was popular and seemed like a winner. He was careful to demonstrate that he was in some respects an admirer of Thatcher and viewed with disdain Major's 'weak' leadership. Tory newspapers showed interest in Blair from the beginning, and non-Tory newspapers and their columnists were excited at what they saw as the dashing radicalism that he seemed to espouse. The media enthusiasm felt new and different. There had been nothing like it for a Labour leader since the early years of Wilson, who had also found ways of seeming 'modern' and of personifying the 'future' in a manner that excited the newspapers.

Blair also seized the constitutional agenda to claim distinctiveness. Soon after becoming leader, he developed what appeared to be close relationships with two key

figures from outside the Labour Party. Blair's assidu-
ously cultivated rapport with the leader of the Liberal
Democrats, Paddy Ashdown, and his friendship with the
former Social Democratic Party (SDP) leader and Labour
cabinet minister Roy Jenkins triggered a huge amount of
media speculation about a realignment in British politics
that might transform the political landscape. Ashdown's
compelling diaries from the period when Blair became
leader to the 1997 election show that the Labour leader
met his Liberal Democrat counterpart on a one-to-one
basis more often than he did most shadow cabinet members. A formal committee was established comprising
senior Labour and Liberal Democrat members to explore
options for constitutional reform. Some shadow cabinet
members were worried that they would not get prominent
positions in government, and would be replaced around
the cabinet table by Ashdown and other Lib Dems. Their
worries and the wider speculation about a transformed
political landscape fuelled the sense that 'change' was on
its way.

Blair's friendship with Jenkins caused at least as much
of a stir as his relationship with Ashdown. Blair did not
turn to former Labour Prime Ministers for advice. In
fairness, by 1994 Harold Wilson was unavailable, ill with
Alzheimer's. But James Callaghan was very much around
and discreetly resentful that Blair did not seek to learn
from his experience or that of most of the former Labour
cabinet ministers who were still alive. They were 'old

Labour' in the recalibrated world of New Labour. In an interview with me for the *New Statesman*, Callaghan pointed out he was 'original Labour', a polite but heartfelt response to being dismissed as 'old'. Jenkins had left the Labour Party to form the SDP in 1981. By 1994, he was a Liberal Democrat in the House of Lords. Blair was much struck by Jenkins's assessment that most of the previous hundred years had been the 'Conservative century' partly because of the schism on the left. Blair's mission was to make the next century one dominated by 'progressives', healing the split between Labour and Liberals. He made several big speeches on the theme, and asked Jenkins to come up with a report on the best alternative to the first-past-the-post voting system, which a Labour government would put to a referendum. Jenkins enthused about Blair and the Labour leader was equally effusive about Jenkins.

Yet here too nothing was quite what it seemed. Blair was not especially interested in constitutional reform and was privately opposed to electoral reform, the proposition that was central to his relationship with Ashdown and Jenkins. Indeed, uncharacteristically for such a disciplined and focused leader, he was too candid in one pre-election interview. In July 1996, Blair was asked during a long and relaxed on-the-record conversation with the *New Statesman* whether he was in favour of proportional representation (PR):

'I'm not persuaded of the case for PR.'

'Does that mean you're against it?'

'Yes. I have never been convinced that small parties do not then get disproportionate power.'

All hell was briefly let loose when the interview was published, as Blair sought to reassure Ashdown that he was committed to a referendum and that he had not ruled out some form of PR being part of a new voting system. The dance resumed, but when Labour won a landslide it came to a near-abrupt halt, but not wholly. Blair opted for a more proportional voting method to elect the new Scottish Parliament largely to appease Ashdown, who did not get either a place in the cabinet or a referendum on electoral reform. One of the many consequences of this decision was that Labour soon lost its dominance in Scotland. Blair's attempt to please Ashdown provided a massive boost to the Scottish National Party (SNP) as it began to make the most of its representation in the parliament under the wily Alex Salmond. Blair saw devolution as a means of killing off the threat posed by the SNP. The opposite happened.

Blair might have been fleetingly too open when discussing his view on electoral reform, but on the whole his style as an interviewee contributed to a sense of novelty, that he was leading a fresh and new project. In the mid 1990s, the broadcast interview had become the main form of political communication. Speeches at big public events and press conferences were fading in significance. Social media was still to come. The interview was acquiring increasing importance on the main TV channels and on radio. Blair was masterful, conversational while giving the impression of purposeful clarity. One of his techniques was to say to an interviewer: 'If I could lapse into candour for a moment – something a leader should never do...' He would follow up with a comment that was politically entirely safe, such as suggesting that in the past Labour had not always been pro-business but his government would be. The apparent candour advanced his cause. But Labour leaders had often been prickly or insecure interviewees, knowing that one word out of place could bring the entire fragile edifice falling down. Blair could navigate the hurdles.

The biggest actual change Blair brought about before the election was an internal move of symbolic potency. At his first party conference as leader, he proposed a new constitution for the party. In effect he was planning to scrap Clause IV, a section of Labour's constitution that had acquired a mythical status. It endorsed the 'common ownership of the means of production, distribution and exchange'. Some of Blair's predecessors had mocked or openly challenged its relevance, but it had become a symbol of radical ambition for some in the party. Blair needed to show that Labour was 'new' and identified the slaying of Clause IV as a way of doing so. He deployed the authority of his recent victory to sway doubters such as his deputy, John Prescott, and Robin Cook, the Shadow

Foreign Secretary. Full shadow cabinet support was essential. Equally importantly, he spent a considerable amount of time writing a new constitution, including a replacement for the legendary Clause IV that stressed 'our common endeavour... to create... a community in which power, wealth and opportunity are in the hands of the many, not the few'. Such carefully calibrated words aimed at securing the approval of the 'many' gave space for those who hoped for radical change and would not offend previous Conservative voters who might switch to Labour. Party members backed the new constitution at a special conference in the spring of 1995. Labour had become 'new'.

The policies that accompanied the hailing of a 'modernised' party were vague in key areas if they had not been already established under Smith or Kinnock. In the mid 1990s, there was a raging debate about whether the UK should join the euro, the single currency for the European Union. The governing Conservative Party was being torn apart over the issue, with Major under intense pressure from his Eurosceptic wing to offer a referendum before signing up. His Chancellor, Ken Clarke, and Deputy Prime Minister, Michael Heseltine, were passionately opposed to such a move, recognising that the concession would be a bleak defeat for the party's pro-Europeans. In the end, Major succumbed and persuaded Clarke and Heseltine to go along with the policy. Blair mocked Major mercilessly and wittily in the Commons. He looked at the front bench opposite and proclaimed that he agreed with Major's

Chancellor, and then asked the Prime Minister who he agreed with. Major could only waffle awkwardly. Blair responded majestically: 'The difference is I lead my party... He follows his.' In various forms Blair's affirmation has been copied by opposition leaders since.

There was, though, a twist. Blair was in a similar position to Major. He was undecided about a referendum or whether to come out as a supporter of the UK joining the euro. In his more messianic moments, he assumed this would be his historic mission, to end what he described as the UK's 'ambiguous relations' with Europe by joining the single currency. But, at the same time, he did not want to lose the support of Rupert Murdoch and his newspapers, who were passionately opposed. By the time of the 1997 election, Blair had also proposed a referendum, and told *The Sun* during the campaign that he 'loved the pound', while being photographed with a British bulldog. Meanwhile he was deepening ties with business leaders by insisting that he would lead a pro-European government. In years to come, the question of whether Britain should join the single currency would lead to one of his biggest rows with Brown.

Where Blair and Brown applied a distinct 'New Labour' approach to policy, they tended to be extremely cautious while persuading gullible political commentators to hail their 'radicalism'. In January 1997, Brown announced that Labour would stick to the Conservatives' spending plans for the first two years in government and would not revise the current rates of income tax for the first full term. Smith had committed Labour to renationalising the railways; Blair spoke out in favour of privatisation in general, including of the railways. On this Brown concurred, and proposed a further privatisation of air traffic control, partly to show that this part of the Thatcherite architecture would not be challenged. Unsurprisingly, Thatcher, looking on in semi-retirement, declared that her greatest triumph was Blair, a leader of the Labour Party who was paying homage to her boldest ideological venture, the privatisation of many industries that had been in the public sector, although she had been wise enough not to touch the railways. They were privatised under Major.

Caution dressed up as boldness was the pattern. The five promises that formed the party's 'pledge card' at the 1997 election were deliberately incremental, seeking to reassure and offer some hope simultaneously. The pledge on schools was typical. Blair had asserted during an early party conference speech that his main priority could be summed up in three words: 'Education, education, education.' The conference roared its approval. The media could hardly contain its excitement. The pledge card in this policy area stated that Labour would 'cut class sizes to 30 or under for 5-, 6- and 7-year-olds by using money from the assisted places scheme'. The scheme had provided places in private schools for less well-off pupils. Arguably, the main beneficiaries were the private schools themselves, who got the money while being able to claim a connection with the less privileged. The symbolism had a hint of radicalism, but the sums involved were small and the measure, though valuable for those attending slightly smaller classes, was tiny.

Such analysis did not get a look-in in 1997. Blair had conjured up a prevailing sense that he would be the agent of historic change. The end of his party conference speech in 1995 was typical of his oratorical verve:

> It is new Britain, one Britain – the people united by shared values, shared aims, a government governing for all the people and the party, this party, the Labour Party, new Labour, founded by the people, back truly as the people's party. New Labour, new Britain, the party renewed, the country reborn. New Labour. New Britain.

He had made a pitch to the widest possible range of voters seem breathtaking in its excitement. Tired of the long-serving Conservative government, now visibly falling apart, even some Tory newspapers joined in the worship. Only a few close observers expressed their doubts. Blair had a conversation in the build-up to the 1997 election with shadow cabinet member Clare Short, who was frustrated by the caution and what she saw as the influence of aides behind the scenes: 'the people who live in the dark', she once publicly noted. Blair sought to reassure her. 'In government we will be more radical, Clare.' Without hesitation she replied: 'You mean even more right-wing?' Short was both right and wrong. Over time Blair moved further to the right. Yet once safely in power he and Brown implemented a range of policies that transformed the quality of life in Britain while retaining enough support to win two more elections, a unique achievement.

CHAPTER 2

Power

L ABOUR'S victory in the 1997 election was dazzling. Here was a party that had lost four elections in a row not only winning but doing so spectacularly. Tony Blair's majority of 179 exceeded Clement Attlee's in 1945 and Harold Wilson's in 1966, both big wins for Labour. Only Keir Starmer came close to such a landslide in 2024, partly by copying Blair's path to victory. Blair had achieved what he had set out to do, forming an election-winning coalition of voters from across the political spectrum: traditional Labour voters, those who had previously voted Conservative, business leaders, trade unionists, the young and old, north and south, *Sun* and *Guardian* readers. There was a tangible excitement on the night of the election and in the days that followed that was almost without parallel in modern British politics.

In the early hours of the Friday morning Labour's ecstatic formal celebrations took place at the Royal Festival Hall on London's South Bank. 'Things Can Only Get Better' by the pop group D:Ream, Labour's anthem during the campaign, blasted out of the speakers close to the dance floor. Senior party figures, journalists and anyone else who could get hold of an invitation danced excitedly. Around the country there were celebratory parties overnight or across the sunny weekend that followed. Blair arrived shortly after five in the morning from his constituency in Sedgefield and was greeted like a rock star. The sun was rising as he spoke and, always alert to the drama being played out, declared: 'A new dawn has broken.' So used to losing elections, the crowd went wild in response to a political metaphor extracted from the sun appearing above the Thames.

Yet even on the night of an unqualified electoral triumph there were complexities, layers of ambiguity. In his memoir Blair revealed that he regretted almost immediately uttering such uplifting words to open the new era. For all his instinctive evangelical flair, he did not want voters to expect too much from a government unused to power and determined to retain the range of support that had propelled it to its spectacular victory. Following the reference to a new dawn, Blair moved down a gear. He insisted: 'We were elected as New Labour and we will govern as New Labour.' He repeated those words outside Number 10 later that morning, before entering the Prime

Ministerial building for the first time. From day one he was determined to reassure those who had previously voted Conservative that this would be a new project in government as well as in opposition. At the same time, he was warning those who were eagerly anticipating a leap to the left now that they had safely won to forget about such dreams. This was going to be different.

Even the dancers at the Festival Hall could not quite cope with the new political situation, including those who had been directly involved in the transformation. For some reason I ended up on the dance floor opposite Blair's senior adviser David Miliband. As we were gyrating awkwardly, he said to me, as 'Things Can Only Get Better' blared in the background: 'I'm sure we'll wake up in the morning to find the Tories have won again.' On the first page of his memoir, Blair reveals that, as he entered Number 10 for the first time, his 'predominant feeling was fear, and of a sort unlike anything I had felt before'. Such an emotion was unsurprising. He was 43 and had never been in power before in any capacity, and the country could barely contain its excitement that change was on its way.

There was complex ambiguity even about what it was that voters were celebrating. Was it the arrival of what they hoped would be a change-making Labour government under the youthful Blair, or was it the end of 18 years of Tory rule? One of the first books to be published after the election, Brian Cathcart's *Were You Still Up for Portillo?*, contained in its mischievous title a reference to the unexpected defeat of Michael Portillo, then the most prominent cabinet minister on the right of his party. The title captured a delight in the fall of the Conservatives, but there was hope too that Labour would bring about change. As one of Blair's senior advisers, Philip Gould, observed later, the manifesto was cautiously incremental but the election result marked such a break with the past that it created an assumption that sweeping change would follow in terms of policies.

Blair might have felt fear but he had a developed sense of how he wanted to lead. He was elected as New Labour and he would govern as New Labour. What did he mean by this? In terms of an ideological guide Blair spoke of a 'third way', navigating between Thatcherism and traditional Labour policies. President Clinton was the original inspiration behind this idea and joined Blair for seminars on its significance. This was a vague philosophy, an anti-ideological ideology. The nearest equivalent in the UK had been Harold Macmillan's *The Middle Way*, published in 1938. Although Macmillan was a Conservative who went on to become Prime Minister, his view of the middle way was in some respects to the left of Blair's version, showing a greater faith in the role of the state to address inequalities, poor housing and, to some extent, public services. Blair saw his third way as a means of marking a break from Labour's past while being more alert to the need for decent public services than the Tories to his right. The philosophy was conveniently flexible, and Blair remained a devotee, even attempting a third way in the build-up to the war in Iraq. This attachment was one of the many differences between him and Gordon Brown. As Chancellor and Prime Minister Brown never once referred to the third way.

The caution that shaped Blair's pitch at the election continued in government. In the early days of the first term, he told colleagues that the campaign to win the next election had already begun. He intended to do nothing that jeopardised what became known as his 'big tent' of support. He wanted to be the first Labour Prime Minister to win at least two full terms with big majorities. He had every intention of keeping *The Sun* newspaper on board and hoped to secure the approval of others, including the *Daily Mail*. As one cabinet minister noted privately as the 'first hundred days' came to a conclusion: 'We hit the ground reviewing,' with quite a few thorny policy decisions being kicked into the long grass.

Yet within Blair's willingly chosen constraints there was a sense of early hyperactivity. He summarised the carefully planned early initiatives in his memoir. They included, in order of announcements: the abolition of state-funded assistance for private schools, a new Department for International Development, the granting of independence of the Bank of England, the introduction of a new half-hour, weekly slot for Prime Minister's Questions in the Commons (replacing two 15-minute slots), compensation for Gulf War veterans, a reform that enabled National Lottery proceeds to be spent on health and education, a cut on VAT on fuel to 5 per cent, a restoration of trade union rights at GCHQ, bills for referendums on a Scottish Parliament and a Welsh Assembly, legislation for a London mayor, signing up to the 'Social Chapter' of the Maastricht Treaty, the launch of a Low Pay Commission to agree on a minimum wage, a new welfare-to-work programme, and quite a lot more.

Some of these policies were much bigger than others. The independence of the Bank of England was a substantial act of reassurance, Brown giving up his powers to set interest rates in order to free himself of the burden of fears that the markets would strike him down. Labour governments elected with big majorities in 1945 and 1966 never recovered from the trauma of being forced to devalue the pound. By making the bank responsible for monetary policy, Brown triggered a sense in the markets and the media that this would be a 'prudent' government, turning away from levers that might lead to short-term gains while making the economy more vulnerable. Blair was fully behind the move and at times claimed to have instigated the major reform. In truth, Brown's senior adviser Ed Balls had been working on the details in opposition and had advocated the change in a pamphlet published by the Fabian Society shortly before he joined Brown's team. Even so, they had to move quickly. Brown only decided on the step shortly before the election.

The architecture around the bank's independence had been carefully thought through, an example of hard graft behind the scenes in opposition paying off once the election had been won. The elected Chancellor still retained influence, appointing the governor of the bank and members of the Monetary Policy Committee. Brown also set the bank's inflation target, instructing the new masters of monetary policy that inflation should not go above or below 2 per cent. Privately Balls stressed the importance of not going below this amount as much as he did the more obvious objective of avoiding inflation taking off.

The bank's independence was to have many consequences, one of which was to change Brown's views about joining the euro. At times in opposition, Brown had been more enthusiastic than Blair about at least leaving open the option of signing up to the single currency. He was worried that the referendum would be an impossible barrier. As a Shadow Chancellor and with an acute awareness of Labour's history in government, he knew that Chancellors can be fatally destabilised by humiliating devaluations of the pound. Being part of the single currency would remove the threat of sterling being targeted by the markets under his chancellorship. But immediately after the election Brown announced the independence of the Bank of England, an alternative protective shield against market turbulence. He soon saw only the downsides of joining the euro. Blair took a different view, continuing to see joining the euro as part of his historic destiny. Already Blair had within him two differing forces: a self-deprecating, highly focused expediency and a deep sense of mission.

The other early changes were relatively small, did not go to plan or were accidentally radical. The constitutional reform that Blair managed efficiently but without great enthusiasm was the establishment of a Scottish Parliament. The previous Labour government had fallen as a result of its attempts to secure devolution through a referendum in 1979. Blair succeeded in winning a referendum for a legislature north of the border by a big majority and in establishing a degree of consensus over the powers the new body in Edinburgh could deploy. This was an historic reform, and one that an unlikely alliance had warned against. The defeated Prime Minister, John Major, was convinced that devolution would fail and only lead to overwhelming demands for full independence. He spent the last day of the 1997 election travelling around Britain warning that the future of the UK was at stake. A former Labour leader who agreed with him was Neil Kinnock. He had been an opponent in the 1970s and had not changed his mind. Before long they could claim to have had a point. Part of the calculation of those in Labour who were pro-devolution was that the transfer of power would help to kill off any threat posed by the SNP, a party with oscillating support over the decades prior to the 1997 election. Within a few years, the party's leader, Alex Salmond, was First Minister. In 2014, the then Prime Minister David Cameron felt compelled to hold a referendum on independence. Salmond and his fellow supporters of an independent Scotland lost by 55 to 45 per cent, but the defeat proved to be a spur for further campaigning for independence under Salmond's successor, Nicola Sturgeon. Blair implemented the devolution settlement speedily and deftly, but the arrangements were fragile.

Blair's greatest achievement in his first term had not been the subject of pre-election scrutiny, the thousands of articles analysing how the youthful Blair would change Britain. Alongside a lengthy cast of unlikely heroic figures, Blair secured peace in Northern Ireland. John Major had begun the process in the mid 1990s, recognising courageously that there was space to engage constructively with the Sinn Fein leadership, which had come, cautiously but determinedly, to seek a political solution rather than a military one. The calculations of Gerry Adams and Martin McGuinness were layered but also brave. Major was correct to judge that they were being sincere. But he lacked the bandwidth to sustain momentum as his government moved from one storm to another, mostly relating to the management of his party. Towards the build-up to the 1997 election, Major did not have the authority, energy or time to twist and turn with all the relevant forces in Northern Ireland and beyond. In particular, the right in his party was becoming increasingly contemptuous of his engagement with political forces well beyond the Unionists. Blair and his Chief of Staff, Jonathan Powell, recognised before they got to power that in this highly charged policy area they would have the space to act and to pursue an agreement for as long as it took.

The immense task played to Blair's strengths. Almost uniquely, Northern Ireland liberated him from the usual, stressful range of political calculations he had to make in relation to most domestic policies. Was he creating too much room for the Tories to recover? How would the media react? What was Gordon Brown up to? For one thing, the previous Tory government had instigated the peace process, and so Major gave him cover. Furthermore, the London-based newspapers were not as interested in Northern Ireland as they should have been; meanwhile, though Brown was watching Blair like a hawk on a range of domestic issues, this was not one of them. Blair was free to take risks, exercise patience and deploy his immense negotiating skills. There were never-ending meetings with Unionists, nationalists, the Irish government. On all sides stances were taken and dropped. Agreements seemed to be close and then far away. But from the beginning the mood music was in place. Blair's Northern Ireland Secretary, Mo Mowlam, was ready to engage with nationalists in ways that no predecessor had done, thanks to her accessibility and exuberant style. Blair's first Prime Ministerial visit outside London was to Belfast. In a speech on 16 May, he tiptoed adeptly along the trapeze wire:

> I said before the election that Northern Ireland was every bit as important for me as for my predecessor. I will honour that pledge in full... My message is simple. I am committed to Northern Ireland. I am committed to the

principle of consent. And I am committed to peace. A settlement is to be negotiated between the parties based on consent. My agenda is not a united Ireland – and I wonder just how many see it as a realistic possibility in the foreseeable future. Northern Ireland will remain part of the United Kingdom as long as a majority here wish.

He added that he wanted Sinn Fein to join the talks but that the IRA must end the violence. In these carefully woven words, there was space for the parties in Northern Ireland with their conflicting hopes and convictions. For Unionists, Blair was committed to Northern Ireland, and a united Ireland was not a possibility in the 'foreseeable future'. But he hinted that there might be such an outcome if that became the wish of the majority. He set the scene for the Good Friday Agreement signed in the spring of 1999, in which party leaders who had been at war undertook to serve together in the newly established Northern Ireland Assembly at Stormont. Many played their role, but Blair's tireless and deft wilfulness were pivotal. The agreement stands as an historic achievement and made more sense in the wider context of devolution for Scotland and Wales. A Scottish Parliament and Welsh Assembly were established after early referendums that were won. Given that failed attempts at devolution triggered the sequence of events that brought down the last Labour government in 1979, the relatively smooth journey to new power centres in Edinburgh and Cardiff was another sign of well-prepared sure-footedness, even if the consequences in Scotland had not been properly considered.

Such was the apparent confidence of Blair and this first Labour government since 1979 that much of the media started to note an arrogant swagger. The opposite was closer to the truth. Blair and Brown had been brought up on losing elections. They assumed the Tories would soon be back and that in the meantime the government was an impostor disturbing the natural order in which the UK elected Conservative governments. It was one of the assumptions that the duo did share. England was a conservative country that usually backed the Conservative Party. With a big majority neither was arrogant enough.

The respect both paid to their inheritance, the 18 years of Tory rule, is in marked contrast with the Conservatives when they won from opposition in 1979 and 2010. David Cameron did not even secure a majority in the latter election, and yet he and his Chancellor, George Osborne, moved fast in the direction of the radical right. Cameron and Osborne had responded to the global financial crash in 2008 by calling for real-terms spending cuts, the only mainstream leaders to do so across the suddenly fragile world economy. Even the US President, George W. Bush, spent vast sums to keep the financial sector afloat, as did the fiscally conservative Angela Merkel in Germany. Undisturbed by the response of others, Cameron and Osborne proposed cuts in the 2010 election along with a

'Big Society' in which the state did less and other agencies did more. Together, these policies were a form of turbo-charged Thatcherism. They found themselves in a coalition with the Liberal Democrats, but this did not stop them introducing a budget within weeks of the election that implemented their programme of austerity. At the same time, they rushed through plans for fixed-term parliaments and sweeping reforms of the NHS and schools, along with a law that any new EU treaty would have to be passed by a referendum, the beginning of the end of the UK's membership. Here was a government on the right moving at the speed of sound without a Conservative majority in the Commons.

New Labour's changes were less dramatic. Meanwhile the Blair government stuck to Tory spending plans for two years and did not raise income tax, while stepping back from any attempt to tamper with the previous government's extensive and rushed privatisations.

When contemplating immediate policy implementation, Blair was more wary than Thatcher or Cameron. But when looking into the relative safety of the long or middle distance, he was more daring. Almost out of the blue, in 1999 Blair set out a path to end child poverty within 20 years. In a sign of the deep tensions already forming, Brown and his team, admirably obsessed with the challenge of inequality, had no idea Blair was going to make the pledge. Ed Balls, Brown's close senior adviser at the time, told me: 'We heard the speech in amazement as Tony had shown no interest in our anti-poverty agenda... and decided that instead of kicking up a fuss about not being consulted we would use it to get more of our policies past Number 10.' There had been several clashes between Blair and Brown over the latter's focus on tax credits as a way of helping those on low pay rather than on public services. Now they were both committed to poverty targets, and it was in this context that Sure Start expanded speedily, a service aimed at bringing poorer or disconnected families to a range of education and social services, another policy that proved Clare Short at least half wrong. On Sure Start, Blair was much more radical in government than before the election, delivering more than he promised.

Yet the child poverty target was partly tactical, on one level hugely ambitious and on another one that could not be tested, since Blair would not be Prime Minister for another 20 years. Delivering such a speech was both safe and radical, Blair's favourite combination.

Blair set a much more demanding target, and one that could be tested, in relation to the NHS. Halfway through the first term, the NHS had shown few signs of improvement. The government had not increased spending significantly and had few coherent ideas about how the service could be 'reformed'. By the beginning of 2000, the situation was becoming unsustainable. Robert Winston, a famous TV doctor at the time and a Labour peer, told the *New Statesman* that it would be safer for his mother to be treated in an Eastern European hospital than under the decaying NHS. Meanwhile, the *Daily Mail* was campaigning for nurses to be better paid. By instinct, Blair rarely saw higher public spending as part of a solution. But every now and again he came to recognise that there was no other way through some crises than to spend. He had underestimated the scale of the emergency in the NHS, and, when both the *Mail* and Lord Winston were calling for a big injection of cash, he moved fast.

Blair used a TV studio to make one of the most striking and dramatic announcements of his leadership. On Sunday, 16 January 2000, he was giving his regular new-year TV interview to Sir David Frost. The Sunday political programmes became devalued in the years that followed, but at that time *Breakfast with Frost* was a weekly event of some significance. With a flourish, Blair pledged to bring NHS spending up to the EU average by 2006. This would mean increases of around 5 per cent in real terms each year, a huge leap. Blair acknowledged that 'spending is too low at the moment'. He was right and had finally sensed the urgency of the situation. But this was policy making on the hoof and a sign that, by the end of the first term, the government was becoming partially dysfunctional. Blair had no idea how the money would be raised. He did not consult Brown because he did not think that the two of them could have a considered discussion on the issue in advance of the announcement, and that his Chancellor would probably angrily dismiss the ambitious spending proposition.

Indeed, Brown was apoplectic in the aftermath of the interview, for several reasons, not least because Blair got the glory of the popular announcement while he would have to do the hard grind of finding the cash by putting up taxes. He had also not realised the deep crisis in the NHS and had planned more incremental rises. Both Blair and Brown had assumed that a Labour government could not put up taxes on income and survive. They were convinced that the culture around tax and spend in England particularly would make such a move unacceptable. Suddenly, both were in a position where they would have to test such an assumption. They needed a level of investment that only a tax rise on income could generate, an immense project for the second term.

The same haphazard approach applied to Europe. By instinct, Blair was pro-European, indeed the most pro-European Prime Minister since Edward Heath. But Heath's ideas in relation to Europe were deep and fully formed. On becoming Prime Minister in 1970, his task was daunting but clearly defined. Heath wanted Britain to become a member of what was then the Common Market. He achieved his passionate ambition by 1973, succeeding where both Harold Macmillan and Harold Wilson had tried without getting close. For Heath, entry to the Common Market was a high point of a troubled premiership. But, from the beginning, membership triggered turmoil in British politics, dividing parties and before long bringing down Prime Ministers. By 1997, Blair partly recognised that the interests of his party lay in becoming even more tonally pro-European than it had been under Neil Kinnock and John Smith, his two predecessors, both committed Europhiles, Kinnock being a convert to the cause. The Conservatives had fallen apart over Europe, to the despair of business leaders in the UK. Enthusing about Europe matched Blair's desire for Labour to be the pro-business party. He was also wholly at ease with the UK's membership and unbothered by the Maastricht Treaty, which alienated so many Conservatives. He recognised that the UK had to be part of a larger enterprise to compete with the United States, China and other big players in the increasingly global economy.

Blair's view of his leadership in relation to Europe was more ambiguous than Heath's. After the 1997 election, he had left open the option of joining the euro in the first wave, scheduled for 1999. Bizarrely, in the autumn of 1997, following months of unresolved tension between Number 10 and Number 11, Brown's mischievous press secretary, Charlie Whelan, briefed *The Times* from the Red Lion pub in Westminster that an interview the Chancellor had given the newspaper in effect ruled out Britain joining the single currency in Labour's first term. Blair had no idea that this definitive message was to be conveyed, just as Brown had not known that Blair was to announce a big increase in health spending on David Frost's TV sofa.

In both cases they got to the right place in the end, but the process was symptomatic of a freakish power dynamic.

Blair and Brown were the only dominant figures in a landslide government. They held each other to account and that was more or less it, with the inevitable exception of the media, which bothered both. The cabinet accepted unquestioningly the outcome of any battle between the two of them. The House of Commons was largely irrelevant as Blair presided over a huge majority.

There was, though, also a discipline and order to Blair's first term, particularly where media management was concerned, that formed an impressive counter to the chaos that occasionally erupted over big unresolved policy areas. He had the capacity to command unqualified loyalty from those who worked for him in Number 10. Alastair Campbell became almost as famous as Blair, even though he was supposedly his behind-the-scenes press secretary, one of several job titles acquired over the many years during which Campbell toiled sleeplessly. Blair and his predecessor Harold Wilson experienced a similar dark arc in relation to newspapers and the BBC. Each of them enjoyed a highly supportive media at first. They were portrayed as modernisers with a mission. Even Conservative newspapers were not as vitriolic as usual. With its bias for following the fashionable mood as determined by the newspapers, the BBC was also fairly unchallenging to both leaders at the beginning. But, by the end, both Wilson and Blair in their different ways despaired of the media. The newspapers turned on Wilson after the devaluation in 1967 and never became supportive again. After he lost the

1970 election, the BBC broadcast a documentary with the dismissive title *Yesterday's Men*. Given that all those who featured, from Wilson downwards, planned to contest the next election, the title alone was enough to justify Wilson's fury. The substance was as bad, reflecting all the clichés of the right-wing newspapers at the time about a bunch of tired, disillusioned figures from an era that had passed. In 1974, yesterday's men formed a government and ruled until the election in 1979. Meanwhile, Blair's final speech as Prime Minister was an attack on the media, describing it as the 'feral beast'. While Prime Minister, he told me that dealing with the media was like living with a demented tenant whom you were not sure whether to be friendly to or cosh over the head.

Campbell was at the heart of the government because of Blair's preoccupation with the media. Having been brought up politically in the 1980s, a time when Labour endured catastrophic coverage in the media, Blair saw the message as being directly connected to delivery. That delivery would not be recognised by voters if unaccompanied by effective messaging. From his election as leader in 1994, Blair enjoyed a glowing media profile. This was partly down to his own instinctive brilliance as a communicator: humorous, assertive, alert to all dangers and opportunities. But Blair was dependent on Campbell's around-the-clock exertions, wooing some outlets and pressurising others, while framing messages that would work in the age of the sound bite. Blair had known Campbell since becoming an MP in 1983. He had been a rarity at Westminster: an openly Labour-supporting journalist, one who worked closely with Blair and Brown, among others. From the outset, Blair spent more time with Campbell than with any politician or adviser. When not in the same room or building, they were in constant contact. There had been nothing like it before in British politics. Thatcher revered her press secretary, Bernard Ingham, but Ingham was a civil servant, even if he did join the band of Thatcher devotees. Wilson was close to his media guru, Joe Haines, but he had so many other calculations to make beyond his fraught relationships with newspapers and broadcasters that the significance of Haines's presence was limited. Blair regarded Campbell as a genius in terms of his ability to read the rhythms of news stories, including how long a troublesome one was likely to be given prominence and what to do about it. Campbell's hyperactivity ensured a perception of smooth government even if this was not the full picture.

Blair was also close to Peter Mandelson, a relationship formed when Mandelson was director of communications for Labour from the mid 1980s. After Mandelson backed Blair for the leadership in 1994, Brown hardly spoke to him before he brought him back into his own fragile government with a Shakespearean move in 2008. In contrast, Blair remained close, needing Mandelson for what he regarded always as his wise advice and also for his humour. In the midst of a crisis he would look up at his advisers and demand: 'Get me Peter.' Like Campbell, Mandelson was often attacked in the media for being an evil spin doctor. Unlike Campbell, he was an MP by the time Blair became leader and determined to be a minister. Blair appointed him to various significant ministerial posts, but also sacked him twice for noisy but tiny and fleeting misdemeanours. Somehow or another they remained close.

Blair's capacity to be ruthless and simultaneously to generate a sense of loyalty among his closest confidants was an important part of his armoury as a leader. He was not able to apply these important qualities in his dealings with Brown, his oldest friend in politics. Their relationship, the early closeness and later intense differences, defined Blair as a leader and Prime Minister.

CHAPTER 3

Blair Wins Another Landslide

I n 2001 Blair became the only Labour leader to have won two successive landslides, an epic achievement given his party's tendency to lose elections. The victory put him up there with Margaret Thatcher as a winner. Attlee won with a massive majority in 1945, but only scraped home at the following election and was out of power by 1951. Blair had secured at least another full term and remained in full command of the Commons. Blair and Brown also shifted the ground a little to the left in 2001, though nowhere near to the extent that Thatcher had moved her party and country ideologically rightwards in her landslide victories.

Nonetheless, much more than in 1997 Blair and Brown were able to put the case for the virtues of public investment. The main argument of the campaign was Labour investment versus Tory cuts. Admittedly, the Conservatives – now under the youthful, inexperienced leadership of William Hague – fell into a trap. They went into the election offering a 'guarantee' of tax cuts, a policy privately opposed by the Shadow Chancellor, Michael Portillo, and that could only credibly be financed by big reductions in spending. Given that public services were still tottering and Labour's extremely cautious approach to spending in its first term, the prospect of further cuts became a vote-loser. Blair and Brown pledged again not to raise income tax, but they held their ground in relation to National Insurance, despite fleeting demands from the still-mighty *Sun* newspaper for them to rule out increases. Unlike Keir Starmer and Rachel Reeves in 2024, they did not do so. The space to increase National Insurance was to become important in the second term.

Even so, the election was quite subdued. Blair remained a formidable campaigner and was not threatened by Hague. But improvements in public services had been relatively small. There was not a great deal to be excited about. In a characteristically robust exchange on the BBC during the campaign, Jeremy Paxman opened his interview with Blair by making a broadly accurate and provocative observation that Blair could not wholly deny: 'Prime Minister, there aren't enough doctors or nurses. There aren't enough teachers. There are more cars on the road than when you came to power. The train service doesn't work. Violent crime is rising. Is that what you meant by the new Britain?'

The inevitable consequence of sticking to Tory tax-and-spend plans during the first term was limited progress on all the fronts that Paxman highlighted. Blair could only reply by stating: 'We accept there are all sorts of things we still have to do… We've made a start, we've laid foundations.' He pointed out that Labour had delivered on its early pledges but they had been deliberately small. In this interview and others, Blair also stressed the importance of reforming public services by working with the private sector. Paxman asked him what he meant by this. The only example Blair gave was the Private Finance Initiative (PFI) that had paid for the building of several hospitals at considerable long-term cost.

The comparison between Blair's view of 'reform' and Brown's lay at the heart of even deeper tensions between the two in the years that followed. Indeed, the relationship was on Blair's mind during the campaign. During a lull in the election Blair told his close friend, the TV executive Barry Cox, that he had given the impression to Brown that he would stand down during a second term but that he was now resolved not to do so. He knew Brown would fume.* So it turned out. One of the early conversations when both were back in Downing Street revolved around Brown's angry opening question: 'When are you going to

---

* Conversation between the author and Barry Cox during the 2001 election.

leave?' But the rivalry went well beyond ambition. There was also a growing ideological divide.

The relatively subdued nature of the campaign was reflected in the turnout: 59.4 per cent compared with 71.3 per cent four years earlier. Even so, Blair had secured a majority that most leaders dream about. He only lost six seats, returning with 412 MPs and a majority of 166. He was in command of the Commons again, but the next few years were to be as draining as those endured by Prime Ministers with no majority at all.

This was partly because he returned to Number 10 with a crusading sense that 'reform' of public services was his domestic mission. He thought that increased spending was not the solution, even though he had committed to bring spending on the NHS to the European average. Blair was leaving it to Brown to work out how that would be done. In particular Blair became obsessed with changes to the NHS and education. He made his close ally, Alan Milburn, Health Secretary. Milburn was even more effusive about reforming the NHS than Blair: dynamic, charming, eager to please his Prime Ministerial boss, reflective and yet, like Blair, reluctant to reflect too forensically on the consequences of his ideas. Blair appointed the dutiful former teacher Estelle Morris Education Secretary. Morris was decent, without great ego or unyielding ambition. She was perceptive, too. On assuming her new role, she told her senior advisers: 'There are Tony's departments and there are Gordon's departments... We are one of Tony's departments,' an insight into the unusual duopoly that shaped Blair's government, with cabinet ministers dancing to the tunes of Blair or Brown depending on which department they were in. At the beginning of the second term, Blair told Milburn and Morris that he expected them to serve the full term and bring about sweeping changes. Morris lasted for little over a year, resigning in October 2002. Milburn resigned in 2003, famously stating that he wanted to 'spend more time with his family'.

Blair made great play of seeking to 'reform' public services, but there was nothing unusual in such zeal. Every Prime Minister reforms services in one way or another. Attlee's government 'reformed' the NHS that it had launched by introducing prescription charges, a change that triggered the resignations of the former Health Secretary Aneurin Bevan and the future leader Harold Wilson. Structural reforms of the NHS were relatively common under Labour and Tory governments. Similarly, in education, Labour and Tory governments of the 1960s and 1970s had abolished grammar schools and created comprehensives. As Prime Minister, Wilson introduced the Open University. Yet Blair and quite a few political commentators hailed 'reform' as a new phenomenon. Opponents of his version of 'reform' were dubbed 'anti-reform', as if there were only one kind of 'reform' available, when in reality there were many.

Blair's basic premise was incontestable. In the modern era, patients and parents of pupils expected 'choice' and to be empowered to make that choice. The NHS was not especially productive and pupils could be trapped in poorly run schools, poorly managed by local education authorities. In terms of the NHS, he sought a more extensive role for the private sector, not only in meeting demand but in encouraging innovation and efficiencies. He looked back at the reforms introduced by Margaret Thatcher and her Health Secretary, Ken Clarke, that were aimed at establishing an internal market that would deliver better outcomes for patients. As part of the vision interpreted by Alan Milburn, foundation hospitals would be introduced, with much greater freedom to manage their budgets and responsibilities, including the right to borrow on the market and to set their own pay rates.

The 'reforms' triggered Blair's biggest ideological clash with Brown in their entire stormy relationship. In the 2002 budget, the Chancellor had successfully announced a significant tax rise, a National Insurance increase, to pay for the biggest leap in NHS spending since its formation. Polls suggested that voters approved, to the disappointment of editors of Conservative newspapers who had commissioned the surveys. But in the immediate aftermath, Blair was keen to press on with his changes. Brown's objections were partly practical and partly political. After taxes had been put up, what would happen if a foundation hospital went bust? How could patient choice be delivered without the surplus capacity at the best hospitals so patients could opt to be treated in them? If there were to be surplus capacity, what would be the response of the *Daily Mail* and others to hospitals being 'half empty'?

More fundamentally, Brown had a deeper sense than Blair about when markets worked and when they did not. In a speech delivered in 2003, Brown pointed out:

> In health, price signals don't always work, the consumer is not sovereign, there is a potential abuse of monopoly power, it is hard to write and enforce contracts, it is difficult to let a hospital go bust and we risk supplier-induced demand... If we were to go down the road of introducing markets wholesale into British healthcare we would be paying a heavy price in efficiency and equity and be unable to deliver a Britain of opportunity and security for all... Equality of access can best be guaranteed not just by public funding of healthcare, but by public provision.

Allies of Blair dismissed the argument as 'anti-reform', but the words were a statement of the obvious in relation to a service free at the point of use for anyone who might fall suddenly ill or who had long-term health needs. In the end, Blair conceded quite a lot of ground to Brown, limiting the power of foundation hospitals, revisions that were a factor in Milburn's decision to resign. Where Blair persisted, the outcome was mixed. As Brown warned, introducing private suppliers proved expensive and required new layers of bureaucracy to arrange. But when this was combined with the needed investment, patients began to see marked improvements in healthcare, from speedy access to GPs to modern treatments for serious conditions without long waits. Under Blair, polls suggested approval ratings for the NHS were at their highest ever. But the battles between the two top figures were draining and, as in the case of the disagreement over investment in the health service, went way beyond the familiar soap opera of personal ambition. In his otherwise convivial memoir, Ed Balls, then Brown's most senior adviser, describes the row as being 'as much as Iraq... the New Labour tragedy'. He was right. A noble, unified desire to revive the NHS was blown apart by an avoidable internal split at the very pinnacle of government.

In education, Blair also looked back to an extent at some of the reforms introduced during the Thatcher era. As we saw in Chapter 1, before becoming Prime Minister he declared that his passion could be summed up in three words: 'Education, education, education.' In the build-up to the 1997 election, in another somewhat simplistic assertion, Blair insisted he was concerned with 'standards not structures', failing to recognise that structures inevitably partly determine standards. But, by the beginning of his second term, he was bothered about structures. The new head of his policy unit, Andrew Adonis, drove a fresh set of reforms that included the introduction of city academies at secondary level, schools removed from the control of local authorities. Adonis was so passionate that when he became schools minister in 2005 the academies were in effect accountable to him. He set them up and followed them closely. But such ministerial assiduousness was not always going to be possible, especially when the number of academies and self-governing schools increased. Then there would be new questions about scrutiny and accountability.

Blair's bigger battle was in his determination to introduce theoretically variable tuition fees of up to £3,000 a year. Initially, Brown was opposed and encouraged his allies in the parliamentary party to rebel. His preference was for a graduate tax, fearing that those from poorer backgrounds would be deterred from going to university. But, at the last moment, the Chancellor indicated support for the proposal and urged his allies to back off. Even so, Blair won the vote in January 2004 by only five votes. Brown could have defeated him and inflicted a near-fatal wound to his Prime Ministerial authority. He resisted because, with his leadership ambitions in mind, he did not want to be associated with another tax, or to appear as the insurrectionary Chancellor. He was trying to find ways of indicating that he would be different from Blair, but not so different as to alienate newspapers, such as *The Sun*, that continued to back Blair. Brown never found a successful way through this dilemma.

During the rows over public service 'reform' Blair thought about standing down. His memoir is a telling, though one-sided, guide to the psychodrama, of which there had been no equivalent in British politics. Blair writes in a way that seems admirably balanced:

> Was it reasonable of him [Brown] to block measures
> simply because I would not yield to him the position of
> prime minister? Of course not. But then look at it from
> his point of view: constantly waiting; constantly fretting
> that I might sacrifice all political will before the crown
> was his; constantly fearing the passage of time.

Brown's position was slightly more nuanced than that. He was not blocking measures only because Blair wouldn't leave Number 10, though that was a factor. He and his advisers had genuine doubts. Yet the relentless aggression from Brown and his senior advisers did lead at times to a form of stifling paralysis within government, so that Blair had every right to despair. Some of Blair's advisers, including his Chief of Staff, Jonathan Powell, urged him to sack Brown. Blair came close but made the right call not to do so. As he generously acknowledges in his memoir and in many interviews, Brown was a formidable Chancellor. No one else could have met such titanic demands in the same way. Also, Brown on the backbenches would have been at least as dangerous as he was in the Treasury.

Blair claims in his memoir that he contemplated resignation but only if Brown agreed to continue his programme of reform: 'So if he will only agree to carry it through, why not put the burden down, get out, escape?' But Blair's thinking was a trap for Brown. He could not commit to adhering wholly to Blair's view of 'reform' because he genuinely did not agree with it all and feared that full implementation could lead to electoral defeat. Blair equally sincerely believed the opposite, that only by sticking with what he regarded as the essence of New Labour, a project that was on neither the left nor the right as far as he was concerned, could the party win. He also believed passionately in the efficacy of the reforms.

Blair goes on to write his version of a dramatic meeting with Brown in November 2003 – chaired by his deputy, John Prescott – in which he offered to resign.

> I said I needed to know that he would be one hundred per cent committed to the reform programme and would carry it through after I left. He said of course he would. John [Prescott] came back in [he had briefly left the room]. I said: I have made it clear I won't serve a third term and will go before an election, but I need Gordon's full and unconditional support.

Here was another ambiguous exchange as the two of them danced around the issue of leadership, a conversation that had begun in the summer of 1994. Blair appears to be agreeing to what Brown had assumed he had said before. He would be gone by the end of the second term. Yet once again the condition was one that Brown could not wholly meet, even if he said he would as part of this latest negotiation. As Blair puts it: 'I have put it down baldly. He would say: I received an assurance Tony would go. I would say: I received an assurance Gordon would cooperate and carry through the agenda.'

As Blair acknowledges, the exchange was based on a dangerous assumption: that the allocation of power was to be decided by the two of them alone. It was another example of the degree to which the duopoly had seized control of Labour and then the government. He blames Brown's sense of entitlement. But the framing is flattering for him. On this basis he is not concerned about personal ambition but only for the noble cause of 'reform'. When he realised Brown would not deliver his vision, he had no choice but to continue in Number 10 for the sake of the country. Only he could deliver. This was also a form of rationalised entitlement, useful for Blair at a time when his weaknesses were exposed by what was happening in relation to Iraq, the dark saga that was running parallel to these intense domestic battles. Many British Prime Ministers face impossible dilemmas and mountainous challenges. Heath, Wilson and Callaghan were all laid low by the traumas of governing in the 1970s. But no modern Prime Minister had endured pressures such as those on Blair since Anthony Eden fell from power over the Suez crisis that erupted in the summer of 1956. Eden was gone by early 1957. Despite the exchange in November 2003, Blair was far from gone. The autumnal meeting resolved nothing. Blair concludes: 'the feelings on [Brown's] part of entitlement... burgeoned still further from that moment on.' Their relationship continued to deteriorate.

Nonetheless, Brown's sense of entitlement was not wholly unreasonable. Blair's reforms were not as indisputably necessary and thought through as he suggests. When David Cameron became Prime Minister in 2010, he tripled the cost of tuition fees, to the opposition of even ardent Labour advocates such as Adonis. Such a mechanism was only available to him because of the policy implemented during Blair's second term. Cameron's reforms of the NHS were presented, partly accurately, as building on Blair's. The end result was a fractured NHS that led to even Tory Health Secretaries, during and after the Covid crisis, arguing that there had been too much fragmentation and that a greater degree of centralisation was required. After Iraq there were also raging questions about Blair's integrity, which were largely unfair. Brown had cause to worry that the longer he waited, the more the entire government would become infected. As they met in November 2003 and subsequently, there was also some basis to his sense of entitlement in that no other Labour candidate would have won a leadership contest. It was Brown's crown to seize, but only if the holder stood down.

Blair continued to contemplate resignation until another meeting with Brown in May 2004, prompted by concerns that the Treasury was resisting his 'five-year plans', programmes that looked well beyond the next election. Again, the resistance was understandable in that Brown would be in charge of implementing them and, once more, he had doubts about some of the ideas behind them. No

Chancellor had ever put such pressure on a Prime Minister to leave. No Prime Minister had sought to ensure his successor was bound to his ideas and policies for years to come.

Two of the smartest politicians in Labour's history had become blind to their own follies, while each obsessed over what he saw as the other's fatal flaws. Blair's confidence in his own leadership abilities and insights rose perversely after the nightmare of Iraq. On one level he was astute enough to recognise that the invasion had been a calamity, but he also had the capacity to convince himself that it was the 'right thing to do' and that he was now a leader who took decisions irrespective of their popularity. As we shall see, this was not the case even in relation to Iraq, where Blair sought what he considered to be the least thorny route only to discover he could not navigate it. Subsequently, he played the leader who was all-knowing in relation to public service reform, the economy, security and the state of party politics. But even in such a post-Iraq state of mind, Blair should have been able to see that it was not for him to bind the hands of a successor for years to come.

Meanwhile, Brown had become so tortured by the need to be Prime Minister at the earliest opportunity that he failed to see how his behaviour was perceived. He had potential allies in Number 10 in his ideological disputes with Blair, but alienated them all and intensified their sense of loyalty to the Prime Minister. His hunger for the top job was too transparent, and his determination to succeed without a proper leadership contest – a 'smooth transition' – did convey a sense of entitlement, betraying an assumption that it was up to the two of them to decide where power lay. In their different ways, both saw so much about how to win and govern a country conditioned to be wary of Labour. Yet they saw so little as their battle reached fever pitch.

In the autumn of 2004, Blair pursued his most aggressive moves. He made his close ally Alan Milburn head of strategy and policy. Brown and his senior advisers loathed Milburn. In otherwise guarded private conversations with journalists, Brown spat his surname out with venom. Brown had been central to the election campaign in 1997 and 2001. With the appointment of Milburn, Blair was suggesting that the next campaign would be altogether different. Shortly afterwards, Blair told the party conference in Brighton that he would serve another full term but would not seek to contest the election after next.

Again, the dramatic words, announcing a departure but not for years, were framed solely with Brown's ambitions in mind. A form of madness followed. At the start of the new year, the election year of 2005, both Blair and Brown made speeches on international development at precisely the same time. Mischievous broadcasters juxtaposed them on the screen. In January, journalist Robert Peston published a semi-authorised book on Brown that had been written on the assumption that he would be

Prime Minister, or close to being, at the time of publication. The book contained further explosive revelations about Blair and Brown's relationship, with Brown quoted as saying that he could not believe a word Blair uttered. These transparent tensions followed Blair's decision to chair a political cabinet on the forthcoming election while Brown was abroad.

Perhaps inevitably, there was a twist. In the build-up to the 2005 election, polls suggested that Brown was significantly more popular than Blair. The ratings reinforced in Blair a sense that he was now 'doing the right thing', irrespective of the polls. Even so, the likes of Alastair Campbell, now out of Number 10 but still in near-daily contact with Blair, and the polling guru Philip Gould, who was also close to the partially resolute Prime Minister, became convinced that a rapprochement between the two of them was essential. With Blair's permission, Campbell and Gould held a series of meetings with Balls and Ed Miliband to find a way through. They succeeded, though only just. In effect, Brown would run the campaign while broadly endorsing Blair's reforms, which were to be at the heart of the manifesto.

There continued to be moments of heightened tension. During the campaign Blair and Brown filmed an election broadcast together in an attempt to convey a continued unity and harmony. Though used to affecting unity in public, they struggled to pull off this particular act. In another campaign event, Blair bought Brown an ice cream.

The two of them did not look as if they were eager friends on holiday. Yet they held it together. At joint press conferences, when Brown was asked to back Blair on Iraq and public sector reforms he did so. Blair hailed his 'brilliant Chancellor'. The Tories, under the leadership of Michael Howard, a former cabinet minister on the Eurosceptic right, were more polished than they might have been, but they struggled to land a glove on the fragile duo.

Blair won again, though Labour now had an overall majority of 66, much smaller than the previous two landslides. On one level, it was the greatest electoral achievement of the three: usually, Labour governments did not last very long. This one had secured a third term. But clearly the tide was turning under Blair's leadership. The still-chaotic Conservatives secured more votes in England than Labour. Blair did not enjoy the campaign. He faced constant questions about his integrity in the aftermath of Iraq. Being constantly asked whether he lied to go to war was not a particularly flattering theme. During the campaign I interviewed him on a train between Birmingham and London; he said that he wished he had published the raw intelligence in relation to Iraq, thereby avoiding the huge row that erupted over Number 10's dossier that aimed to show definitively that the country's dictator, Saddam Hussein, possessed weapons of mass destruction (WMD). That quarrel might have been avoided, but the tentative nature of the intelligence might also have undermined Blair's awkward case for war, the theme of the next chapter.

Meanwhile, Howard chose to focus on immigration in ways that inevitably made the campaign more highly charged than those of 1997 and 2001. Immigration was the theme of his opening speech. At one stage, Howard proposed to move illegal asylum seekers to an unspecified island. 'Where is this island?' Blair asked. By 2024, a Conservative Prime Minister was proposing to fly them to Rwanda as the theme of borders and those seeking to live in the UK became an ever more explosive policy area.

During the second term, some of the government's significant successes were only indirectly connected to Blair and were, sometimes, in spite of him. Blair was a great advocate of mayors, but blocked Ken Livingstone from being the Labour candidate in the London contest. But Livingstone became the first elected mayor, winning as an independent. His subsequent introduction of the congestion charge reduced the number of cars coming into the city while raising revenue for public transport. Over time, the Underground and buses were transformed. Blair had the agility to admit in public that he had been wrong about Livingstone. Other cities were also improved significantly. Sure Start continued to play a key role in improving the opportunities for poorer families. One teacher at a school where most of the pupils were from poor backgrounds, a person on the left of the Labour Party, told me for a newspaper feature at the time that the government had helped to improve the lives of those she taught dramatically. She became a Blair supporter.

Blair also gave the go-ahead to civil partnerships, the prelude to same-sex marriage, later introduced by the coalition government elected in 2010. Civil partnerships were the necessary precursor to the bigger leap, clearing the path by formally legitimising gay relationships. The reform was an echo of the social changes instigated by Roy Jenkins when he was Home Secretary in the late 1960s, implemented against the background of some noisy protestation but with cross-party support. The change endured and was built upon. There has been no attempt to reverse the sequence. As with Jenkins's reforms, civil partnerships did not feature in election campaigns, nor were they part of the focused internal discussions, or rows, about the future of the Labour Party. Although socially liberal, Blair was not gripped by social issues as he was by the need for his version of public service reforms. Nonetheless, he did not stand in the way. He saw the reform as another 'third way', partnerships rather than marriage, and recognised that the compromise would not risk alienating too many social conservatives in middle England, whom he regarded as an essential part of his coalition of support. Like the smoking ban in public places introduced in his third term, the reform had nothing to do with 'tax and spend', the dominant theme in British politics, but had historic consequences.

But for Blair, the second term was dominated by Iraq, the seemingly never-ending attempt to convince his party, the media and the wider electorate that his approach was the right one, and then the even more draining efforts to justify the bloody consequences, made much worse when no WMD were found. Many feared Blair had become dangerously messianic. He had not changed at all.

CHAPTER 4

Iraq

TONY Blair's approach to politics was formed largely in the 1980s, with Labour's failures to get close to winning an election and, equally important, Margaret Thatcher's glittering dominance electorally and in terms of her authority over her government. A source of strength for Thatcher was the perception of her as an 'Iron Lady' in relation to foreign policy, after she became a war leader and her popularity grew. Indeed, from the Falklands conflict in 1982 until the war in Iraq in 2003, there was a widespread assumption that military action involving the UK would be broadly popular and enhance the standing of a Prime Minister. After Thatcher's victory in the South Atlantic, some newspapers, the Conservative Party, sections of other parties and a lot of voters celebrated without much reason what they saw as the return of the UK as a major global force. The mood in the country seemed closer in spirit to the victory in 1945 than the humiliation of Suez in 1956 or the economic doldrums of the 1970s.

After the war in Iraq, a different set of questions were posed. What was the UK doing there? Did Tony Blair lie to the country to justify war? Was he too weak to challenge President Bush? Blair moved towards Iraq burdened by Falklands-era assumptions and orthodoxies only to discover that they were now outdated. He had become trapped by the past.

An attempt to explain why Blair went to war in 2003 highlights the degree to which his own dark and complex journey was determined as much by the recent history of his party as by events in Iraq and the wider region, or by an unruly US administration. This journey began soon after he became leader of the Labour Party. During his first party conference speech in the autumn of 1994, he announced the need for a new constitution. While Blair was preparing this, he received a note from his close friend Peter Mandelson. The two of them had been exchanging ideas on the final wording of the important new document. Mandelson noted that there was no significant phrase about defence policy. He shuddered at the absence, his memories still painfully vivid of the 1980s, the era when Labour was seen as being 'soft on defence'. The text had little to say about a range of policy areas, this being a statement of the party's broadest values rather than an election manifesto. But Mandelson was aware that defence had been a highly charged vote-loser for so-called 'old Labour', and therefore merited a special mention in the new constitution. 'Will a Blair government not go to war?' Mandelson wrote across the page of the draft and sent it back to Blair.

By this, Mandelson did not mean that a Labour government would indeed seek to go to war. Like the rest of the leadership at the top of New Labour, he had little interest in foreign affairs beyond a passion for Britain's membership of the European Union. His thoughts were related solely to domestic politics. Like Blair, he was conditioned at all times to be alert to Labour's weaknesses, actual and perceived. As the rewriting of the constitution was an exercise aimed at showing that the party had changed, Mandelson was worried that, if there were no reference to defence policy, critics might conclude that Labour was still 'soft' in this area. Blair knew exactly what he meant and followed his advice. In the party's revised constitution there are few mentions of specific policy areas, but defence is included. Blair added the words: 'Labour is committed to the defence and security of the British people.'

Three and a half years before Blair became an MP, Michael Foot, a committed unilateral nuclear disarmer, was elected the party's leader. During his time in that role, Foot joined Campaign for Nuclear Disarmament (CND) marches, as he had done for the previous three decades, speaking passionately against retaining nuclear weapons under any circumstances. Foot deployed some arguments that had merit and were to seem less extreme several decades later, but once they had been mediated through Britain's still-mighty newspapers he was made to look like a dangerous romantic, wholly untrustworthy with the country's defence policies. To plaster over internal divisions during the 1983 election, the leadership came up with the absurd hybrid that Labour was both a unilateralist and a multilateralist party. Blair proclaimed his support for unilateralism as a Labour candidate in Sedgefield, but never believed in the policy. His disbelief was irrelevant. Candidates are obliged to speak for a party programme whether they believe in it or not. Of much greater significance was the way the policy and the equivocations around it caused Labour harm and were cited widely in the pro-Tory newspapers as a reason that the party was unelectable.

However, Robin Cook, who became Blair's first Foreign Secretary and who subsequently resigned from the cabinet over the war in Iraq, pinpointed the starting point of Blair's journey towards the war as being a little earlier than the 1983 election. Blair had been a Labour candidate in the unwinnable seat of Beaconsfield, the first by-election to be held after the Falklands War in 1982. Cook recalled Blair telling him that everywhere he went during that campaign voters were hailing Thatcher's military victory. Cook believed that somewhere in Blair's mind an assumption formed that voters expected British Prime Ministers to be ready for war and that victory would greatly enhance their reputations.

In the 1980s, Labour struggled to get beyond a muddled policy that diminished its reputation. An equally committed unilateralist, Neil Kinnock replaced Foot after Labour lost by a landslide in the 1983 election. While the new leader bravely began to challenge and reform his party against impossible odds, he retained more or less the same approach to defence policy as Foot up to the 1987 election.

As Kinnock continued to resist change in relation to unilateralism during his first term as Leader of the Opposition, a pivotal event occurred, one that was vividly in Blair's mind when he became leader. In March 1987, weeks before that year's general election campaign got under way, Kinnock paid a visit to Washington. The timing had been carefully chosen from his point of view in the hope that a meeting with President Reagan would help him to appear Prime Ministerial.

The precise opposite happened. In a calculated snub, Reagan saw Kinnock for the minimum time protocol demanded. The US administration allowed only a photo of the meeting to be released. The documents from Reagan's archive explain why. In one briefing for Reagan, prepared by his senior officials in advance of Kinnock's visit, the President was urged to stress: 'Labour's position on defence would make it difficult for any American administration to carry on as before. Your policies would have a profound, unpredictable effect on NATO, East–West relations and bilateral relations.' The rest of the briefing was equally scathing about Kinnock and his leadership.

The contrast at the time with Margaret Thatcher was striking. While Kinnock was being cold-shouldered in the United States, Thatcher, the Iron Lady who was perceived to have helped bring freedom to parts of Eastern Europe, was being lauded in Russia. She was treated like a rock idol in Moscow and beyond. But the more vivid and precise contrast was with Thatcher's visits to Reagan, in which she got the VIP treatment no other leader secured, and enjoyed something close to a love-in with the most powerful leader in the world.

In their cramped office at Westminster, Blair and Brown watched the media coverage of politics like hawks, in particular the reporting of Kinnock's weaknesses and strengths. They drew a single conclusion from Kinnock's visit to Washington and the inevitably exaggerated derisory coverage from the British media: a Labour leader is credible only when he or she has a close relationship with the US President. Thatcher had become an international star and more leader-like at home partly because of her very special relationship with Reagan. Kinnock had become less leader-like and electable because he was given no more than a few minutes at the White House.

Labour lost again in 1987. Thatcher won once more by a landslide. In Kinnock's second term as Labour leader, defence policy again became a form of hell. He asked his Shadow Foreign Secretary, the wily Gerald Kaufman, to achieve the big switch from unilateralism to multilateralism, but the process was draining and traumatic. Kinnock suffered from exhaustion and depression, and contemplated resigning. Nonetheless, he succeeded in changing the policy on nuclear weapons, a titanic achievement given the still-powerful internal bodies that had to give assent. Indeed, in one interview Kinnock was asked: 'As leader of the Labour Party you are reviewing the party's commitment to unilateral nuclear disarmament, but what is your personal position?' Kinnock laughed and replied: 'Having personal views as leader is a contradiction in terms. As leader of the Labour Party I don't have personal views.' The words merit a book on their own. A leader is often so constrained that his or her personal views cease to be relevant.

But even though Kinnock had changed the policy to one that was more explicitly multilateralist, he still struggled with questions relating to defence. Persistently he was asked whether he would be willing as Prime Minister to press the nuclear button. He equivocated. In a speech to his party conference in 1986, admittedly before the change from unilateralism, he came closest to a formula with which he was comfortable: 'I would die for my country, but I could never let my country die for me.' This implied that nuclear carnage would follow if he pressed the button, but that he was personally willing to fight for his country. It was not a sign of personal weakness or cowardice that he was reluctant to trigger nuclear meltdown. Nonetheless, Kinnock was torn apart by the media, struggling to keep his party united over the issue and tormented by his personal journey from committed unilateralism, and most voters only detected weakness.

In the 1992 election, the Conservatives and their newspapers made endless references to the support for CND of Labour candidates including Kinnock, even if by then the leader and others had moved on. Labour suffered a fourth successive defeat. There were many factors that contributed to Labour's inability to win general elections. Perceptions of weakness in relation to defence appeared to be one of them. At the very least, given media hostility, the stance reinforced the views of most voters that Labour was not fit for government.

In the run-up to the 1997 election, Blair was absolutely clear where he stood in relation to defence policy. There was no evasion, ambiguity or equivocation. Labour's past led him towards apparent clarity. At a press conference on foreign policy in the spring of 1997, he was asked whether as Prime Minister he would be willing to press the nuclear button. He replied without hesitation: 'Yes.'

Like Mandelson in his intervention in the discussions over the party's new constitution, Blair was not thinking of taking part in a terrible nuclear conflagration. His unqualified response was a symbolic act. He needed to purge his party of its immediate past: Foot's unilateralism and Kinnock's contorted evasiveness. In a clear, accessible manner he had to show he would be strong on defence.

In one of the many Shakespearean twists en route to Iraq, Blair's determination to stride away from Labour's vote-losing history led him towards a war that would be at least as contentious and damaging to his and his party's reputation as any of old Labour's perceived misdemeanours.

Several biographers of Blair have accused him of being messianic about the removal of Saddam Hussein soon after arriving in Number 10. This makes no sense. He knew little about Iraq and the region. He was commendably gripped by the need to improve public services and was obsessed with winning a second election. Iraq was always on his mind, but for a different reason. Throughout his leadership, successive US administrations were contemplating or threatening military action in the country. How would he respond? From the day he arrived in Number 10 in May 1997, a new leader with no great knowledge of or interest in Iraq and the wider region, he was alert to the question and the need to find an answer, as well as being determined to be seen to be different from previous Labour leaders. This was his guide towards how he would answer the persistent question about military action in Iraq.

From his early months as Prime Minister, he knew that President Clinton was contemplating an attack on Saddam. What would he do in such circumstances? He was a New Labour Prime Minister, not an 'old' one. He was close to Clinton. In his mind he had no doubt about where he would be if the President chose to strike. He would support his close ally, the most powerful leader in the world. The sequence of thoughts that led to Blair's unequivocal conclusion were not triggered by a detailed study of Iraq, but a sense of what was expected of a New Labour Prime Minister.

In February 1998, Blair paid his first visit to President Clinton as Prime Minister and was treated like a superstar. Three and a half years earlier, he had been a relatively obscure Shadow Home Secretary wondering if his party would ever win again. Now he was making waves as Prime Minister in the United States as the President's closest international ally.

Blair's visit became famous because it coincided with the highly charged peak of the Monica Lewinsky saga. The alleged affair between Clinton and Lewinsky was a sensational theme at the joint press conference between Clinton and Blair in Washington. Did Clinton have an affair with Lewinsky? The question was posed in different forms several times by US journalists as the two leaders stood side by side. Wholly obscured since and ignored at the time, the other topic of the press conference was military action in Iraq. This was the chosen topic of the two leaders, not what Clinton had got up to with the young White House intern. No one noticed. The BBC headline after the press conference was 'Blair backs Clinton over Lewinsky allegations'. The UK newspapers were similarly gripped. But Iraq is what Blair had prepared for in advance of his visit. Lewinsky was not a challenge for him. In contrast, he regarded what he said on Iraq as a huge early test of his leadership.

Clinton had started to become obsessed with Saddam.

His critics assumed that the obsession was a convenient diversion from the Lewinsky saga. Perhaps they were right. Whatever his motives, Clinton could not have been clearer in his introduction to the Washington press conference with Blair:

> The best way to stop Saddam from developing an arsenal of nuclear, chemical, and biological weapons and the missiles to deliver them is to get the inspectors back to work with full and free access to all relevant sites. But let me be clear: if Saddam does not comply with the unanimous will of the international community, we must be prepared to act, and we are.

Blair followed with a precise echo of Clinton's opening comments and with some detail about Britain's readiness for action. In tone and to some extent in substance, he had begun his march towards the war in 2003.

> We have of course to prepare in case diplomacy cannot work. In view of the situation, we in Britain have been looking at our own military readiness in case a diplomatic solution does not, in the end, prove possible. We have decided to base eight Tornado GR-1 aircraft in Kuwait, with the full agreement of the government of Kuwait. These are ground attack and reconnaissance aircraft. Their deployment is a precautionary measure, and it will take place over the next few days.

So all the way through, in respect to Iraq, we've agreed that we must educate; we must engage in diplomacy; but we also must prepare.

Why was Blair so gripped by what was happening in Iraq rather than, say, Bosnia? He was gripped because President Clinton was gripped. He knew he might face a decision on military action and he knew he would support Clinton.

Subsequently much was made of an observation Blair made to the Liberal Democrat leader Paddy Ashdown in November 1997, as reported in the second volume of Ashdown's illuminating diaries. Referring to the intelligence Blair would have read for the first time as a Prime Minister, and without any previous ministerial experience, he told Ashdown: 'I have seen some of the stuff on this. It really is pretty scary. He is very close to some appalling weapons of mass destruction... it's deadly serious.'

The quote has been used as evidence that Blair was always sincerely alarmed by Saddam and that his alarm was based on intelligence. This analysis is flawed. Blair was getting intelligence from trouble spots around the world, including Bosnia. He seized on the specific intelligence from Iraq as evidence to build his case for military action, or, to be more precise, to support Clinton, who was planning military strikes. He cited the intelligence to Ashdown because he wanted to keep the Liberal Democrats on board if the moment came when he would stand shoulder to shoulder, Thatcher-like as opposed to Kinnock-like, with a US President. He knew the Conservatives would support him and that was an important part of his calculation, but he did not want the Liberal Democrats to oppose action in a potentially troublesome alliance with the left of his party. He wanted his big tent to survive a possible military partnership with the United States. Ashdown had been a key figure in the big tent, and Blair wanted him to stay in it. The reference to the intelligence was more than an observation. It was an early act of persuasion, the first example of Blair citing intelligence to make a case. He had been Prime Minister for six months.

In the autumn of 1997, every calculation for a leader of Blair's mindset pointed unambiguously towards supporting Clinton. They were similar calculations to the ones he would make nearly six years later. All the official inquiries ignore the mindsets of leaders and where a psychological outlook can lead, in the same way that they overlook political context and the way a leader can become trapped by actions and external factors. But it is by exploring these areas that we can find the answer to the question of why Britain went to war in Iraq in 2003.

Consider the factors that determined Blair's early support for Clinton's military strike on Iraq. He was a different type of Labour Prime Minister, one who would not shirk tough decisions, including military ones. He was Clinton's closest ally. The Conservatives would support any military action and Blair did not want to give them the space to look more 'responsible' as an opposition than the Labour government. The newspapers, especially those he cared about, would support military action. Labour MPs would be supportive, partly because they admired Clinton. Furthermore, Blair wanted at some point to win a referendum on the euro, so it was important as far as he was concerned to show that he was pro-American in order to build up credit with Rupert Murdoch, whose newspapers he knew would be ready to attack him. Politically, there were no downsides.

Blair had no idea whether Clinton would actually strike, but he prepared the ground. He had never read intelligence reports in great detail before. The world of intelligence was entirely new to him. Some Prime Ministers had experience of such reports before getting to Number 10 as a result of previous ministerial posts, or, as cabinet ministers, had observed other Prime Ministers handling such complex material. Blair read the reports as a novice. He had never been a cabinet minister, let alone one as senior as a Foreign or Home Secretary. Such senior ministers get used to reading intelligence with a degree of scepticism. Blair saw it from the perspective of knowing that he might have to put the case for supporting President Clinton.

On 17 December 1998, US and British forces began a four-day bombing campaign against Iraqi command centres, airfields, weapons storage facilities, and radar and missile sites. Eighteen months into his premiership, it was Blair's first experience as a war leader, one that he had prepared and psyched himself up for. In a statement after the bombing had begun, Blair told the Commons: 'There is no realistic alternative to military force. We are taking military action with real regret but also with real determination. We have exhausted all other avenues. We act because we must.'

The statement was disingenuous. In the view of many other world leaders, the timing was arbitrary and connected more to providing a distraction from the Lewinsky scandal, which was still traumatising Clinton. Blair acted knowing that he would have the near-universal support of MPs and the British media. He was the only other world leader to offer active military support for the strikes. In doing so he was widely hailed as courageous in the British media, kept his big tent intact and purged Labour of its perceived weak-kneed reputation. Here was a Labour leader who could authorise military action with Thatcher-like resolve.

The action went nowhere. There was no follow-up from Clinton and therefore there was no follow-up from Blair. Saddam remained in place. The erratic dance with UN resolutions and UN inspectors continued. Clinton's attentions moved on and therefore Blair's attentions moved on. He had passed his first major test as a Prime Minister, supporting military action, proving a staunch ally of the United States and securing strong support in the UK across the political spectrum.

No cabinet member dissented from the attacks. The Foreign Secretary, Robin Cook, was wholly supportive.

The International Development Secretary, Clare Short, did not demur. The US President was a Democrat. The military action was limited. And, of course, this was early in the life of the government. No minister was going to resign over an attack on Iraq instigated by President Clinton early in the initial term of the first Labour government for nearly two decades. The political appetites of new ministers were still far from sated. Meanwhile, ambitious Labour MPs were not going to rebel when they ached to be ministers. Blair was not the only politician making multilayered calculations. They all were.

The military action was both pointless and a dark warning. Other EU countries were opposed. The pro-European Blair was in favour. The Conservatives were eagerly supportive. In following the instincts and military timetable of a US President, Blair was both mighty war leader, New Labour-style, and yet weakly responding to a US initiative and military timetable over which he had little control.

In April 1999, Blair made a speech in Chicago setting out his 'Doctrine of the International Community'. It was widely seen as his distinct, personal approach to intervention. Subsequently, Blair, his admirers and his critics cited the speech to justify whatever argument was being advanced, as if the address were the product of intensive thinking. This was another misreading.

In fact, most of the speech had been written quickly based on notes from Professor Sir Lawrence Freedman, who was astonished to hear his hastily assembled thoughts become the basis for an entire Prime Ministerial approach to matters of peace and war. A few days before the speech, Jonathan Powell had asked Freedman to produce some reflections. Freedman did so, linking Saddam and Serbia's Slobodan Milošević as challenges facing the international community, and listing five factors to consider in relation to possible military action. Blair made the same connection and recited the five factors as if they were the outcome of his own long, considered deep thinking. Here is what Blair said, his words derived from Freedman's notes in relation to conditions that must be met for military action:

> First, are we sure of our case? War is an imperfect instrument for righting humanitarian distress; but armed force is sometimes the only means of dealing with dictators. Second, have we exhausted all diplomatic options? We should always give peace every chance, as we have in the case of Kosovo. Third, on the basis of a practical assessment of the situation, are there military operations we can sensibly and prudently undertake? Fourth, are we prepared for the long term? In the past we talked too much of exit strategies. But having made a commitment we cannot simply walk away once the fight is over; better to stay with moderate numbers of troops than return for repeat performances with large numbers. And finally, do we have national interests involved?

Not only was the doctrine rushed and based on a single hasty contribution from an admittedly distinguished academic, the words were also evasive. The doctrine could have been deployed to justify not intervening in Iraq in 2003 on the grounds that diplomatic options had not been exhausted. The words left Blair with a protective shield. He could cite the doctrine to justify taking military action if the United States decided to go to war, or not to do so if the United States took a different course. No doubt he also believed in the words. Few could not do so in the abstract.

The subsequent liberation of Kosovo, brought about above all else by Blair's hyperactivity, made a deep impression on him. In domestic policy, Blair had Gordon Brown breathing down his neck every day. Separately, he bore the 'scars on his back' from his early attempts to reform resistant public services. But in Kosovo he had grateful parents naming their babies after him and chanting their appreciation when he visited. For Blair, the war in the Balkans seemed to tick all the boxes. He showed once more that he could be a war leader. The Conservative leadership could do little more than express its admiration.

And then there was the substance that brought about the comforting political patterns. Kosovo was liberated. He had made a difference and, as in Northern Ireland, the desire to improve lives wrecked by violence acts as a counter to the views of those who detect crazed malevolence. As a bonus, Blair had achieved this without the interference of Brown. For once, he had pulled levers and there had been clear responses.

Virtually every day of his premiership Blair had kept an eye on what was happening in Washington, making sure he was more or less singing from the same hymn sheet, often using the precise words of Clinton or Bush as if they were his own. When terrorists attacked the United States on 11 September 2001, he knew instinctively what to do, hardly needing to pause as he switched from the role of British Prime Minister working on a solid but unspectacular agenda to that of global leader.

From 1994, when he first became Labour leader, he had been in training for such an historic moment. If he had been Clinton's closest ally for the ill-thought-through bombing of Iraq in his first term, he would most emphatically be Bush's firmest friend in the light of an unambiguous tragedy, a terrorist attack without precedent on the United States.

Blair was in Brighton ready to deliver a speech to the TUC, largely about the virtues of the euro, Britain's joining of which was to be the historic mission he had in mind for his second term. In fact, by then the case for signing up had weakened considerably, but his need for an act of momentous significance had deepened. The speech was never delivered. Instead, he spoke briefly and with sparkling eloquence about the threat posed by new forms of terrorism and then quickly left the hall.

He and his team rushed back to Number 10 and engaged with Washington with an intensity and persistence that was never going to be easy to sever. Not that Blair wanted to make such a break. The only option for a Labour Prime Minister, as he saw it, was to be close to a US President, any US President.

The adulation that greeted Blair when he visited New York and Washington later that month became a trap. How could he ever step aside from this post-9/11 administration after such a coming together? There were many other important and substantial calculations as the relationship between Blair and Bush intensified in the immediate aftermath. By being close to the United States, Blair exercised a degree of influence in the timing of the inevitable attack on Afghanistan and in his argument that a new international coalition could be formed to address the terrorist threat. There were some in the unruly, divided Bush administration who wanted an early strike on Kabul. Blair was one of those who urged a short delay. His advice was continual, expressed in calls, in personal notes and on that visit to the United States, in which appreciative adulation exceeded anything that Thatcher had experienced. Superficially, Blair was offering advice to Bush, but it was in the context of unquestioning support for military action in Afghanistan. The advice was peripheral in relation to the big military call, which was to follow what President Bush had already decided.

From a domestic perspective – and there is always a domestic perspective for elected leaders to consider – Blair had a new *raison d'être* as Prime Minister. Gordon

Brown's demands for him to go ceased for the time being. The Chancellor was at the margins of another mission for the Prime Minister, who was fast becoming an international superstar. The new Tory leader, Iain Duncan Smith, paid homage to Blair's leadership, privately and publicly expressing his admiration for what he took to be the Prime Minister's courage. Such was the focus on Blair, the election of the new Tory leader was not the main news story even on the day the result was announced. IDS was elected in the shadows and never emerged fully into the limelight of the political stage. Most in the media hailed Blair's principled courage and leadership. The second term that had seemed a little lifeless in the immediate aftermath of the election had acquired for Blair a sudden and distinct sense of purpose.

In January 2002, Bush used his State of the Union address to outline his theory on what he called the 'axis of evil'. This was a pivotal event, the moment when Blair knew that war in Iraq was probable as far as the US administration was concerned. The Taliban had been removed from Kabul with relative ease and Bush wanted to move on. There was little focus from Bush, and therefore from Blair, on how to prevent the Taliban from regrouping around Kabul or how to retain the unity of the remarkable international alliance that had arisen after 9/11. Instead, it was clear that Bush had his eyes on Saddam.

The impatience of the Bush administration to move from Afghanistan to Iraq was without reason or logic. The switch would divert military resources from Afghanistan when the new regime was far from secure. Saddam was an enemy of al-Qaeda and therefore would not be part of the new threat that the United States was supposed to be confronting. Indeed, al-Qaeda would welcome the removal of Saddam. A consistent message of intelligence reports from the United States and the UK was that an invasion of Iraq would heighten the threat posed by terrorists. Instead, Bush declared: 'States like these [including Iraq], and their terrorist allies, constitute an axis of evil, arming to threaten the peace of the world.'

It was the framing of the global challenge as an axis of evil that confirmed for Blair what he always knew was likely. Bush was moving on to Saddam. As he always had done with a US President, Blair moved on too, deploying almost exactly the same words in describing the threat posed by the Iraqi dictator. Blair's wholly supportive response to Bush's speech was revealing. He was a lawyer. He had always framed arguments to help him advance his case. In relation to the 'axis of evil' speech, Blair could have cast his forensic gaze and challenged the assertions made. He was smart enough to do so. Was Saddam arming 'to threaten the peace of the world'? As it turned out, he was not arming at all at that point, but even if he had been, were the consequences enough to threaten the entire world? Who were Saddam's 'terrorist allies'? They did not include al-Qaeda, whom Blair and Bush were supposed to be targeting. Whatever his other ambitions, was Bush that sure Saddam was developing nuclear weapons? It is not difficult to hear Blair frame a sceptical response with a combination of oratorical passion and lawyerly questioning. If a left-wing leader, perhaps from Chile, or a nationalist leader in Russia had made the speech, provoking opposition from a US President, Blair may well have raised such pertinent questions. But it was President Bush who was making these casual assertions. Immediately, without wider discussion in his cabinet or beyond, Blair supported them and started looking for evidence to back them up.

But this time he had to be careful. There would be no automatic political consensus, as there had been in relation to the earlier, more moderate strike on Iraq. Bush was widely loathed in the Labour Party, whereas Clinton was an admired leader, and a significant section would be opposed to war in Iraq. Blair also knew that that section would be a lot bigger if Bush acted unilaterally, without seeking the support of the UN.

After the 'axis of evil' speech, the issue of Iraq started to dominate British politics. As far as Blair was concerned, it had never really gone away since he became Prime Minister. It would never go away again. As ever, he sought a third way, but one that even the navigator of the Northern Ireland peace process could not follow without getting desperately, pathetically lost. From early in 2002, the dilemmas facing Blair were deep, complex and not explored at the time or subsequently.

After hearing Bush's speech there was no question from Blair's point of view that he would remain the President's closest ally. Of course he would. The determination to do so was his deepest instinct. He could only breathe politically in a comfort zone in which he was as close to the US President as Thatcher had been and in which there was no space for a Conservative Leader of the Opposition to make hay.

What about the substance of the issue? Even for Blair, who acquired a reputation for evangelical interventionism, the case for removing Saddam was not absolutely straightforward. How could it be? It does not take a genius to recognise the risks of invading another country, even without exploring the complex composition of Iraq too deeply. Yes, Blair saw the case for removing Saddam. He had convinced himself long ago, when he became Prime Minister, that he was a tyrant who was a threat to international security. He had seen the benefits of 'liberation' in Kosovo. But the proposition that war in Iraq was obviously the way forward was not one about which he could be 100 per cent sure. He was much more certain about the political imperative.

After the attacks of 9/11, Blair read the Qur'an in an attempt to understand why fundamentalists sought guidance from the text. But he was not a specialist on Iraq, its history or the politics of the wider region. He never sought to be one, although he was a quick learner. If he had become an expert, he would have discovered too many complexities and ambiguities about Iraq and what might happen if a tyrant were removed. It was better not to know.

But as a political leader Blair could not imagine opposing President Bush. Indeed, it takes quite a leap to contemplate the alternative scenario: Blair standing up at a press conference in Number 10 and declaring that he disagreed with Bush, the leader he had spoken to so many times since 9/11, the leader he had rushed over to visit after the events of that day, the leader he had worked with as they went to war in Afghanistan. This scenario is impossible to conceive even now, when the calamity of what followed is known. Blair was not going to walk away over a presidential desire to remove a tyrant.

What would he have said if he had decided to break with Bush? Again, it is impossible to imagine Blair uttering these words: 'Until now I have worked closely with President Bush as we faced together the threat posed by terrorism. Sadly, I cannot support the President's depiction of Saddam and his plans to remove him. Instead, I join the French President and the German Chancellor in urging him to reconsider his plans. I know the Conservative leader disagrees with me, and some in my party do too, those to whom I am normally closest. I know also that some newspapers are attacking me for opposing President Bush. But I have no doubt it is the right thing to do.'

There is not a political bone in Blair's body that would have allowed him to make such a statement or any words close to it. He broadly agreed with Bush's view of Saddam. He would never allow himself to be seen to be in alliance with Germany and France against the United States, in a military conflict in which the end result might be the removal of a murderous dictator. He would be horrified at the idea of Iain Duncan Smith being given the space to become Bush's ally while he moved closer to the position of vote-losing Labour leaders of the past, becoming a leader distant from a mighty President. He would be equally horrified by the thought of some newspapers turning on him for failing to stand by Bush in what the likes of Rupert Murdoch regarded as a noble enterprise that would make the world more secure. He would lose the support of Murdoch, and that would be long before his planned referendum on the euro, still his historic objective, the policy that would place him in the history books and the one that he knew would for sure face opposition from the right-wing press.

But as he planned his response to the 'axis of evil' speech Blair knew that securing support for Bush's military adventure within parts of the Labour Party would be extremely problematic. This is what troubled him after the State of the Union address. Bush was a right-wing Republican and widely dismissed in his party and beyond as recklessly stupid. One of the reasons Blair had removed Robin Cook from the Foreign Office was his fear that Cook would not want to work closely with a US administration of that kind. Cook was a pro-European socialist who loathed Bush's politics. Blair replaced him with the more expedient Jack Straw, a figure who reflected more deeply on policy than he did, but who was much less troublesome than Cook might have been. In this new context of a possible conflict with Iraq, Blair knew that parts of his party and possibly some in his cabinet would be deeply alarmed that he was still being supportive of Bush. He was not remotely bothered by the prospect of opposition from the so-called hard left, which was inevitable, but he knew he had to keep as much of his party with him as possible, and, in particular, most of his MPs.

He knew the Conservative leadership would back him, an extremely important element in the equation. If the Conservatives had opposed the conflict he might not have acted as he did. Similarly, if Murdoch's papers had been opposed he would have had more doubts about his determination to be Bush's unswerving ally. A bigger political figure, more courageous, less burdened by his party's vote-losing past, a deeper thinker, might at this point have foreseen what was going to happen in Iraq and moved away from Bush. But the scale of the dilemma was such that moving away from the US President might have risked a different form of hell, at least for Blair. Blair faced a nightmarish decision. If he had declared his opposition to Bush at this early stage, Labour's Atlanticist wing would have despaired. Mighty newspapers would have turned away. The Tory leadership would have been given a distinct position. There was no easy course for a

Labour Prime Minister in early 2002, the period when the course was set. And when it was there could be no going back. Later, angry voters would ask in TV studios why Blair ignored the demonstration, held in February 2003, against UK military action, the biggest in modern times. Some fickle newspaper columnists wondered why he was so determined to press ahead. The answer is that by then he was trapped. He could not stand up and state that he had changed his mind. That would have been more disastrous for him than staying the course. The key decisions were taken a year before.

Here is what Blair had decided as he set out to meet Bush at their fateful summit at the President's ranch home in Crawford, Texas, in the spring of 2002. There was no way a leader of Blair's character was going to turn away from Bush and he had resolved not to do so. What that meant in the aftermath of the 'axis of evil' speech was for the time being conveniently imprecise. Bush had not declared war on Saddam in the speech, merely hinted that this was his plan. So, at this point, Blair was backing Bush in the President's assessment of the threat posed and in his determination to address it. But this was quickly going to trap him.

In advance of his key meeting with Bush in Crawford in March 2002, Blair came up with a characteristic route forward. His plan was not a risky aberration but one wholly consistent with his cautious approach to politics in which he sought to find a position that commanded the widest possible support.

Here was Blair's third way in relation to Iraq. He calculated rightly that most of his party, including the likes of Robin Cook, would support military action if authorised by the UN. At the same time, he assumed that Bush would be seen as a less villainous character if the US President could be persuaded to pursue the Middle East peace process while planning an attack on Iraq, and a renewed focus on the peace process was a virtue in itself. Above all, Blair needed time to build up support for dealing with Saddam. If Bush acted quickly, he would not have the time he needed.

Of course, there was more to Blair's calculations than the need to secure a wider coalition of support. His key adviser, Jonathan Powell, was among several figures who urged him to work closely with the United States to exert some influence. The Bush administration was in danger of becoming a superpower disengaged from allies and international institutions. By supporting him, Blair gave Bush no choice but to engage.

But for Blair, the political context was also key. We know this because if he had simply been concerned to see Saddam removed he could have let Bush and his administration get on with it. Senior figures in the United States were irritated by Blair's involvement and did indeed want to proceed with toppling Saddam unilaterally. Blair could have let them.

The Crawford summit in March 2002 has been the subject of endless speculation. After their private discussions,

Bush announced that he would take the UN route when before it appeared that he was ready to act alone and had viewed the UN with impatient disdain. This was solely because of Blair, who persuaded him to go to the UN when he might have caused an even greater international crisis by attacking Iraq and bypassing the institution entirely. This was a significant shift from Bush, one that annoyed his Vice President, Dick Cheney, and his Secretary of Defense, Donald Rumsfeld, who were impatient to strike and at times found the British Prime Minister an irritant preventing them from doing so.

Bush viewed Blair differently. He knew that invading Iraq was quite a leap and could hardly believe that this supposedly left-of-centre Prime Minister was proving to be so supportive at every juncture. When the two of them were together at press conferences, Bush, a transparent public figure, could not altogether disguise his bewildered disbelief that he had chanced upon a leader who could articulate a case for military action more effectively than anyone in his administration, including himself. Bush was willing to go to the UN knowing that his loyal ally would be with him whatever happened.

Blair secured this change of approach from Bush by making clear that he would be constant as an ally, taking part in military action with the United States if the UN route failed to deliver their joint objective, the removal of Saddam. Blair also pressed the importance of the Middle East peace process as fundamental in securing long-term stability for the entire region. We know he did because Bush started to mention it in vague terms.

After their private conversations, the two leaders held a brief press conference in Crawford. Blair stated revealingly: 'This is an opportunity for the UN to rise to its responsibilities and not to evade those responsibilities.' The words were classic Blair, and formed part of a pattern going back many years in domestic politics. In 1996, he told a local government conference: 'As a government we will give councils more power as long as those powers are used responsibly.' Trade unions would get 'fairness not favours', he said. 'Labour would join the euro when it is in the national interests to do so while the Conservatives would oppose entry even if it were in our national interests.' The statements appear assertive, but in each case gave Blair huge amounts of wriggle room. What did Blair mean in relation to the UN? In the post-Crawford statement he was suggesting that Bush would go to the UN to put his case – a new development – but that the UN must respond by agreeing to pass a resolution that would allow Bush to deal with Saddam. If it did not do so it would have evaded its responsibilities and he would remain in alliance with Bush.

In effect, Blair declared publicly in Crawford that Bush was putting an overwhelmingly powerful case to the UN when he might not have bothered, and the UN should behave responsibly by supporting him.

As the war approached, Bush would regularly hail Blair as 'a man who sticks to his word'. The constant reiteration was never explored at the time. The words could have only one meaning. Blair promised to stand with Bush when military action became necessary and he had done so.

Blair's success in persuading Bush to seek a new UN resolution in relation to Iraq had several profound consequences. Above all, it meant that for both leaders the route to war would focus on the WMD that Saddam was supposed to possess, and indeed, from Crawford onwards, Blair and Bush had to frame their case in relation to that threat. The UN might support the removal of weapons. It would never sanction the removal of a leader. Before Crawford, it was probable that Bush would strike Baghdad openly, arguing that Saddam must be toppled. Blair had stopped an act of illegal unilateralism from a US President. But in doing so he became dependent on an argument about the need to remove Saddam's WMD.

The second consequence for Blair was that he had to prepare for the possibility of military action and to dance to a military timetable largely determined by the United States. At Crawford, Blair partly bought more time to make his lawyerly case in the UK. He knew he could pledge his ultimate commitment to military action because he would have the support of Conservative MPs and, he calculated with less certainty, most of his MPs. He had just won another landslide election. The power of patronage would persuade some doubters. A lot of Labour MPs were Atlanticists who would actively support the venture.

Around-the-clock advocacy soaked up nearly all his efforts in the months that followed. He had no choice but to become an advocate, advancing a one-sided case in the build-up to war. He had voters, the media and parliamentary colleagues to persuade. But in persuading he had little time for practical reflections on what would happen in Iraq after the war. As significant, this passionate act led subsequently to a raging debate about 'trust' and integrity.

September was the most important month in the build-up to war: this was when the act of persuasion began in earnest, with publication of the dossier on Saddam's alleged possession of WMD. Blair's monthly press conference too was dominated by the issue. In retrospect, events of this month were to be viewed differently. At the time, it was starkly obvious that Blair was putting a case. Like all advocates he was selecting the evidence in order to do so. He was chairing a seminar on how best to deal with Saddam. But later he was accused of deception and lying, as if he had claimed to be a neutral communicator of the 'facts'.

Here was a Prime Minister putting a case for the need to act. On the whole, the media concluded that there was nothing surprising in the document, as did those politicians who were opposed to military action in Iraq. Nonetheless, some of the newspapers went over the top in their reporting. The dossier included a claim that Saddam possessed WMD that could be deployed within 45 minutes of an order. The document did not specify against which target. However, Number 10 did not seek to correct subsequent reports in newspapers such as *The Sun* that the weapons could be targeted at British bases on Cyprus, a claim that quickly morphed into the popular belief that mainland Britain itself was at risk. Such a warning from the newspaper that obsessed Blair more than any other was part of the act of persuasion. If Blair were conducting a seminar he would have urged caution in relation to such assertions. But as an advocate putting a case he was delighted at such coverage, hoping it might help change the public mood.

After the war the dossier became totemic, the publication an act of deception by Blair and his press secretary, Alastair Campbell. Reading it subsequently is a darkly comic experience. Every single item of intelligence, presented without qualification, proved to be wrong. It contained a number of allegations that Iraq possessed chemical and biological weapons, and even alleged that the country had reconstituted its nuclear weapons programme.

Plucked out of context, the dossier is shocking. But let us return it to the context in which it was published. Blair had become dependent on the intelligence asserting that Saddam possessed WMD. He wanted UN backing and the intelligence was his ammunition. Justifiably, journalists demanded that if the intelligence was so alarming Blair must publish it. 'When are you going to publish the intelligence?' was a constant question at his Downing Street press conferences. The publication became a pivotal event, one in which Blair had to convince his MPs, the media and the wider electorate that the intelligence justified moving towards war. Within Number 10, the dossier was seen as a case for war, an act of advocacy.

Blair and his advisers were not alone in this assumption. In 2011, Major General Michael Laurie, one of those involved in producing the dossier, wrote to the Chilcot Inquiry – the public inquiry into the nation's role in the Iraq War that was held between 2009 and 2011 – saying that they had known 'that the purpose of the dossier was precisely to make a case for war, rather than setting out the available intelligence, and that to make the best out of sparse and inconclusive intelligence the wording was developed with care'. On 26 June 2011, *The Observer* reported on a memo from John Scarlett, head of the Joint Intelligence Committee (JIC), to Blair's foreign affairs adviser, released under the Freedom of Information Act, which referred to 'the benefit of obscuring the fact that in terms of WMD Iraq is not that exceptional'.

If Blair had been a free agent, he would probably have backed Bush in the toppling of Saddam, bypassing the UN. The Conservative leader, Iain Duncan Smith, had said he would support the United States if they went to war without seeking fresh UN resolutions. But Blair was leader of a party committed to international law as determined partly by UN resolutions. So the intelligence became paramount. The dossier was signed off by Scarlett and the JIC. Later, the BBC claimed that the document had been 'sexed up' against the wishes of senior intelligence officers. Yet those officers had in fact given the go-ahead for publication.

There was one big, pertinent question arising from the dossier. Why was the intelligence so wrong? For all the qualifications surrounding the assertions in the raw intelligence, there was still enough of it to suggest that Saddam possessed WMD. The question was rarely posed. Instead, soon after the war the questions focused on Blair's integrity. Why had he lied? Iraq was a turning point on many fronts. One of the most important was the breakdown in trust.

Yet the answer is that he did not lie. He placed preposterously excessive weight on intelligence that was obviously unreliable. He did so because it had become the only route to war that might allow him to retain his big tent of support. Having taken the decision to publish the information, Blair's sole worry in advance of the dossier was that the public/media reaction would be one of indifference: 'We knew all this already... This does not justify war.' So the dossier was an attempt to dramatise the intelligence in order to make an impact. Blair might have had doubts about some of it, but at that moment he could hardly say: 'Obviously some of this might turn out to be wrong.' He was not in a position to be nuanced. Weakly, he had promised Bush that he would stand shoulder to shoulder with the United States, and he was using every weapon available to him to make that pledge one that commanded wide support.

Blair can be accused of being out of his depth, making shallow judgements about the complexities of Iraq and the wider region, of not being bold enough to challenge Bush (although such challenges would not have changed US policy). But it is wholly wrong to frame the position he was in by the autumn of 2002 in terms of his integrity. That framing has not only made it impossible to form a considered view of Blair's leadership but polluted British politics. More than ever, this vacuous but dangerous slogan is asserted by voters: 'You can't trust those bloody politicians. They even lie to take us to war.'

The scale of the trap Blair was in was laid bare with the passing of UN Security Council Resolution 1441 towards the end of 2002, an apparent triumph for the UK that was in fact a deadly defeat. The resolution text was drafted jointly by the United States and the UK, the result of eight weeks of tumultuous negotiations, particularly with Russia and France. It stated that Iraq would face 'serious consequences' if it did not fully cooperate with the weapons inspectors. The consequences were not specified. If the resolution had stated clearly that one was international military action, it would not have been passed. Blair failed to secure a second UN resolution – he never stood a chance – and could not wait any longer. The reason he could not do so had nothing to do with his own impatience. Blair had proved he could be as patient as was humanly possible in his dealings with the Northern Ireland peace process. But, in that process, he was in charge. He could wait if he felt that that would make a solution possible. Now he was operating on a US military timetable. It was he who had kept the United States waiting. He could not turn to Bush and say, one more time, 'Look, we might get France on board at a future date.' Bush, who had grown to like Blair, would have lost patience. He did give Blair the option of pulling out of the planned military action. But although such a move would have thrilled the growing numbers opposed to the war in the UK, it would have ended forever his alliance with Rupert Murdoch and with those voters who saw him as a different type of Labour Prime Minister, one who was strong on defence. Had he recalled UK troops on the eve of war, he would have been seen as 'weaker' than Michael Foot or Neil Kinnock. For Blair, it was not an option he could contemplate for a nanosecond.

But what about the voters, quite a lot of whom appeared to oppose the war? Without a second UN resolution he knew he would face significant opposition within the Labour Party, and, although he would obviously have preferred to have more support, he calculated that he could manage the dissent as long as most Labour MPs continued to back him. But he was surprised by the size of the demonstration. On Saturday, 15 February 2003, a freezing day, up to a million people marched against the war in London, descending from all parts of the UK, a protest of unprecedented size.

The march marked the most important moment in Blair's transition from a leader who ached to be popular to one who sought a new rationale for his leadership. In response to the astonishing images of the march, Blair declared he did not 'seek unpopularity as a badge of honour but sometimes it is the price of leadership and the cost of conviction'. These are the most important words Blair uttered in the entire Iraq saga. He had apparently metamorphosed into a leader who was guided by evangelical belief irrespective of popularity.

But leaders are human beings. They do not change from one fully formed person to another. They are who they are. These words were uttered by a leader who, when faced by a smaller demonstration of the Countryside Alliance a few years earlier, was so alarmed that he sent his Environment Minister on the march, even though the marchers were protesting against the government. Poor old Michael Meacher, the minister in question, had to join the protest directed at his own administration. But Blair wanted to signal that he understood the concerns of these middle-England types. One of them was the abolition of fox hunting. So keen was the Prime Minister to respond to their worries that he contrived measures to abolish the blood sport that in fact allowed it to continue. Now, faced with a march of a million people on a much bigger issue, Blair was seemingly defiant, the crusader who did what he believed to be right.

Blair posed as the strong war leader, when in reality he was in a weak position, obliged to follow a US military timetable while needing to appear as if he were in control of all that he surveyed. In fact, he was partial master of only two elements of the creaking vessel on which he had set sail long before, the cabinet and the UK Parliament. He knew that the United States would wait no longer to begin military action and he was also impatient for the hell of the build-up to end. Between the days when the UN route closed and the start of the war in March, Blair focused most of his energy on persuading his cabinet to support him and his MPs to vote for a motion backing war. After the conflict, Blair was widely condemned for not paying enough attention to what would happen afterwards, both in Iraq and in the wider region. The condemnation is justified in that the postwar planning was shallow and chaotic. But there is a simple explanation for Blair's lack of focus on the aftermath. Quite simply, he did not have enough hours in the day to make the case for war *and* pay assiduous attention to what would come next. The former *Times* editor Peter Stothard was invited into Number 10 to record a diary of the build-up to war. The intense focus, written sympathetically, was on the final political junction. What would Gordon Brown do? He declared his support for war, but Blair was not sure of his intentions until he made a public statement. Could they persuade Clare Short to stay in the cabinet? Blair managed to keep her in the tent (for a while). What would be the impact of the resignation of Robin Cook, the only cabinet minister to quit his post in advance of war? Could he persuade the majority of Labour MPs to support the war? The aftermath could wait.

As far as Blair was concerned, the invasion went more or less to plan in the short term, as it was bound to do. Step back from the intense politics of the year that had preceded the war and it is clear that it was always going to be a one-sided conflict. Far from being courageous, Blair had chosen to fight alongside the world's only military superpower against an ageing tyrant. There was only going to be one winner of the immediate conflict, and Blair had assumed that, once Saddam was toppled, the controversy about what happened before the war would be forgotten about in the light of another military triumph.

Once Saddam had fallen, Blair had assumed that, at worst, he would not be too badly damaged and, at best, he would get a 'Baghdad bounce' to compare with Margaret Thatcher's 'Falklands factor', one that made her electorally invincible. Voters quickly forgot that it had been Thatcher's errors that had opened the way for Argentina to invade the Falklands. Instead, they had supported her from the moment she sent the task force to win the islands back, and now hailed her victory. The same applied to Iraq, as Blair had assumed it would. This column from Tim Hames, published in *The Times* on 7 April 2003, was typical:

> Not only is the war going well, but domestic disasters have been avoided. On the morning after his unexpected election victory in 1970, Edward Heath reputedly looked

at a television set and, observing the pundits chattering, snorted: 'They've told me all week I was going to lose, now they're picking my Cabinet.' Tony Blair could be excused similar sentiments this morning. Seven days ago most commentators insisted that he was on the verge of another 'Vietnam War', today they are absorbed with the domestic aftermath of military victory. How big, they are asking, will Mr Blair's 'Baghdad bounce' be; how long will it last and what will he do with it?

In the *Sunday Times* there was this analysis a few days later, written by Roger Mortimore of Ipsos MORI:

The British participation in the American-led invasion of Iraq was, at the moment it began, possibly the least popular war with the British public of any in which British troops have joined since opinion polls first began. But no sooner had the first shots been fired than public opinion started to swing in favour of British involvement in the war and kept on going. Within a couple of days the polls were finding solid majorities in favour where previously they had found solid majorities against, a movement which even reports of civilian casualties, 'friendly fire' incidents and later widespread looting and lawlessness apparently did nothing to check. The scale of the change of opinions makes it one of the most dramatic turnarounds that MORI has measured.

The turnaround was confirmed on 29 April, soon after Saddam had fallen. The *Financial Times* reported: 'As the prime minister turns his attention to domestic matters, he will be pleased to receive news that the Baghdad "Bounce" is working well for him... According to an *FT* state of the nation opinion poll, the British are feeling patriotic.'

Once again Blair had navigated the safest political course, however hazardous it appeared to be on the surface. Serving his political apprenticeship in the aftermath of the Falklands War, he was conditioned to assume that wars in the UK are electorally popular if victory is secured. There was never any doubt that the United States would remove Saddam. Sure enough, the war was popular, but only fleetingly. The pre-war demonstration marked a deep change in the country's mood since the Falklands, one that led to a discussion about 'trust' after the war when no WMD were found. This included a blazing row with the BBC that ended with the resignation of the chairman and director general.

More importantly, chaos erupted in Iraq. No weapons were found. Evidence surfaced that suggested US troops had brutally tortured Iraqi prisoners. A bloody civil war took place in the country as various terrorist groups made hay. As opponents of the war had predicted, invasion led to a form of anarchic hell, disrupting the wider region and dividing the international community. They were proved right on all fronts, to the point where it was difficult to find anyone substantial defending the war retrospectively. Blair had to do so. British troops had died. He could never admit that they had done so needlessly, or for a cause that made matters much worse in Iraq and beyond.

CHAPTER 5

Final Term

I N spite of Iraq, Blair won the general election in 2005. Indeed, one of his many calculations in relation to the dark conflict was that supporting President Bush was a more reliable means of protecting his electoral coalition than opposing the planned US invasion. *The Sun* endorsed Labour solely because of Blair's foreign policy, specifically mentioning Iraq in its editorial. The Tories had backed the invasion, so there was no point in disillusioned Labour voters switching to the alternative governing party. His big tent of support had narrowed considerably, but it was still a winning coalition.

After the campaign, Blair returned to Number 10 determined to make the most of what he had publicly declared would be his final term. He had more or less convinced himself that he would be able to lead for another four or five years, resign before the election and make way for a successor, probably Brown, but not necessarily so. He was keen to develop his reforms of the NHS, do more to establish New Labour as the party of law and order, show he was as much a pro-European Prime Minister as well as one who worked closely with President Bush. As he often reflected, he felt he knew how to govern by then even if he was less popular. His self-confidence and sense that the future of the Labour government was dependent on him staying for as long as possible had deepened, despite the raging questions still erupting in relation to Iraq. Indeed, Blair's reaction to Iraq was the precise opposite to Eden's over the Suez crisis. Within months Eden fell ill and was out of power for the rest of his life. Blair felt stronger than ever.

But the facade of unity between him and Brown, fleetingly constructed during the election, was shattered within hours of the campaign drawing to a close. Over the post-election weekend, several Labour MPs called on Blair to name the date when he would step down. On Sunday morning, at what should have been a celebratory moment, the beginning of an unprecedented third term for Labour, I interviewed the former cabinet minister Frank Dobson, a decent politician without a big ego. Dobson loathed personal attacks, but his politics were closer to Brown's than to Blair's. He told me without qualification: 'Tony was an enormous liability in this election... I don't think we can go into important local elections next year... with Tony

Blair as leader and expect to keep many of the councillors we've got now.' Privately, this was the view of Brown's team. They wanted Blair to go within the year. On BBC1, another former cabinet minister, Robin Cook, was almost as blunt:

> The question Tony Blair should be reflecting on this weekend is, having achieved this, having secured his place in the history of the Labour Party and the history of Britain, whether now might be a better time to let a new leader in who could then achieve the unity we need if we are going to go forward.

Cabinet ministers were out and about defending Blair, but the clash was freakish, a victorious Prime Minister under pressure to go in the immediate aftermath of victory. The likes of Dobson and Cook – the latter of whom had previously had a disastrous relationship with Brown, during which the two rarely spoke to each other – had concluded that the Chancellor had been the key to Labour winning the election and that Blair, post Iraq and his contentious public service reforms, had been a problem. Blair's response was to dig in. He was in an unrelenting mood, resolving in his own mind to stay at least until the autumn of 2008.

He had much to keep him busy. Soon after the election he played a significant role in securing the Olympics for London in 2012. The following day, suicide bombers struck London's transport network, killing 52 people. He rushed out a four-point plan, none of them having much, or even any, practical impact. Above all he was working on a party conference speech in which he sought to put his version of New Labour more clearly and daringly than ever before. Blair had become convinced that the response to globalisation was the key dividing line in politics, even if his increasing self-confidence as a prophet in his land was at odds with the views and fears of some of those who lived in it.

Blair always began preparing for his party conference speech months before he was scheduled to deliver it. His speech in 2005 was one of his most personal, outlining his view of the world while making clear that Labour could only win if it agreed with him. This took some chutzpah given that a growing number of Labour MPs were calling on him to go. The speech was his side of the internal battle, one in which he famously explained the inevitability of globalisation: 'I hear people say we have to stop and debate globalisation. You might as well debate whether autumn should follow summer.'

In the years that followed, a huge debate opened up about how to protect communities from some of the consequences of globalisation. Few claimed nothing was possible, that it was the equivalent of trying to prevent the changing of the seasons. But in 2005 Blair was adamant:

In the era of rapid globalisation, there is no mystery about what works: an open, liberal economy, prepared constantly to change to remain competitive... The temptation is to use government to try to protect ourselves against the onslaught of globalisation by shutting it out, to think we protect a workforce by regulation, a company by government subsidy, an industry by tariffs.

The speech dated quickly. Again, in the post-Blair years there was a new focus in the UK and elsewhere on how governments could offer a protective shield against the 'onslaught' without 'shutting it out', whatever that meant. He followed up with a slightly naive section on people's expectations of public services:

The truth is, command public services today are no more acceptable than a command economy. The twenty-first century's expectations in public services are a world away from those of 1945. People demand quality, choice, high standards. Why? Because in every other walk of life they demand them. And they are paying their taxes, so they feel they are entitled to them.

But how to offer people quality, choice, high standards without northern European levels of taxation that Blair opposed and did not believe were necessary? I recall having dinner with the cabinet minister Jack Straw the day after the speech. He made the point that people have a choice of solicitors because lawyers are so well paid there is a surplus of them. Was Blair suggesting a surplus of highly paid doctors and well-equipped hospitals so patients could have a similar choice but free at the point of use? There was then an elegantly written but even more naive passage about the role of New Labour:

> New Labour was first and foremost about disentangling ends and means. Political parties love to tie themselves up in doctrine. They develop comfort zones. Policy becomes ideology, sometimes theology. To challenge it is heresy. To agree it is a sign you belong. But real people in the real world think instinctively, free from doctrine. Not free from values. But free to apply them differently in different times. New Labour reconnected us to them.

Yet means and ends are the essence of politics. Most parties agree broadly on desirable ends, but disagree about the means of getting there. Towards the end of his leadership, Blair sought to extract from his own unusual political journey a global political philosophy. During the following summer, he spoke to Rupert Murdoch's annual conference of executives, staged that year in the United States. He declared that the era of tribal political leadership was over and a new era of 'rampant cross-dressing' on policy had begun. He explained that the divide between 'left and right' was no longer relevant and that the new key division was over 'open versus closed'. This might have been where

Blair found himself after a long period of leadership in which he partly defined himself against his party and its past. But he was making quite a leap to extrapolate from his own position a new comprehensive political vision. Protectionism versus free trade was becoming an urgent issue in the context of the global economy, but divisions over whether to impose tariffs on goods had raged in the nineteenth century as well as for much of the twentieth. The split is a constant theme and was nothing new in 2006. Left and right continued to be the fundamental division, determining attitudes towards the state, taxation, public spending and much more. Blair had been a brilliant reader of the gap between Labour and the electorate in the 1980s. But by the time his own leadership was drawing to a close he was a less reliable narrator, still offering distinct insights with energetic verve but more superficial as he attempted to make sense of his support for President Bush in relation to Iraq, of the claim by the new Conservative leader, David Cameron, to be the 'heir to Blair', and of his own more fragile place in the Labour Party as internal critics began to make their moves.

The doubt within his party reached cabinet level, and well beyond Gordon Brown, after Blair appeared to give unqualified support to President Bush's backing of Israel's attacks on Lebanon in July 2006. There were echoes of Iraq as Blair sought to stand 'shoulder to shoulder' with Bush. In an unusually challenging cabinet meeting, the former Foreign Secretary, Jack Straw, warned Blair that

Israel's actions risked destabilising all of Lebanon. He said he agreed with the Foreign Office minister Kim Howells that it was 'very difficult to understand the kind of military tactics used by Israel', adding: 'They have not been surgical strikes but have instead caused death and misery amongst innocent civilians.' Straw said he was worried that 'a continuation of such tactics by Israel could destabilise the already fragile Lebanese nation'. David Miliband also raised questions about Israel's conduct and whether the UK government should echo precisely the words of President Bush. Both had been staunch supporters of Blair in the build-up to the war in Iraq. A former Labour minister, Joan Ruddock, claimed the party was 'in despair' at the position the Prime Minister had taken, and Ann Clwyd, the chair of the parliamentary party, said that the 'vast majority' of his Labour backbenchers wanted a ceasefire.

Blair was operating above his party in a party-based system. In the summer of 2006, he had told Rupert Murdoch and his top team that political 'cross-dressing' was the new orthodoxy while adopting another contentious foreign policy position, seemingly indifferent to the sensitivities in his party, not least after Iraq. He was alert always to the threat posed by Brown. But beyond that he had become closer in demeanour to a presidential figure, a believer in a new politics that transcended left or right.

But, in the UK system, parties can become assertive, even if it takes some time for them to challenge leaders that appear to have become loftily detached. Towards the end of the same summer, Blair gave an interview to *The Times* in which he refused to give more details about when he would stand down while outlining an extensive programme for the following years. This was the final trigger for the weird sequence of events that led to his fall. The minister Tom Watson, an ally of Brown's, wrote a letter to Blair calling on him to step down. Watson followed it up by resigning from government before he could be sacked. A few other MPs made similar public calls. In his memoir stuffed with candid insights, *Power Trip*, Damian McBride, Brown's press secretary, insists that they knew nothing of the coup against Blair. It did not matter whether Brown's team knew or not. When Blair was fragile, Watson and his co-conspirators made an effective move. Brown followed it up with a stormy meeting in Number 10 in which finally there was clarity as their dance moved towards its final steps. Blair agreed he would announce a timetable for his departure but he would stay for another year. Here was the final twist. At the Labour Party conference in September, Blair made a brilliant, witty, moving farewell speech and, at the end of the annual gathering, returned to Number 10 to continue as Prime Minister. He ruled with the same energetic focus as before but inevitably his colleagues and the media were paying more attention to his probable successor. Brown had been a Prime Minister-in-waiting for years, tormented by Blair's refusal to leave. Increasingly, Blair had been determined to stay, convinced that he alone could successfully implement a

New Labour programme, almost binding a successor to his view of domestic and foreign policy. Instead, he stood down in July 2007, receiving a standing ovation after his last Prime Minister's Questions, his final appearance in the Commons. His final day as Prime Minister was also his last as an MP.

Prime Minister...

CHAPTER 6

Aftermath

B LAIR was a young Prime Minister and a young former Prime Minister. He left office aged 54, still full of energy and a determined self-confidence. He convinced himself he had sought to do the 'right thing' even if that made him unpopular, a theme of his two post-Prime Ministerial books, *A Journey* (2010) and *On Leadership* (2024). The reality was more complex. He consistently aimed to be popular with most voters and the mighty media but towards the end found that the former and parts of the latter had turned against him, at which point he rationalised that unpopularity was a mark of strong leadership.

The arc of Blair's leadership was Shakespearean. When he became Prime Minister, he broke all records in terms of popularity and did so for years. The contrast with Keir Starmer's poll ratings after his landslide victory in 2024 is marked. Starmer and his party enjoyed no honeymoon in the polls in the months that followed the election victory. During the equivalent period, Blair was often 30 points ahead of his main opponents. Yet, when he left office, Blair was so unpopular in some quarters he became an exile in his own land. Public events became close to impossible because of the security demands. The launch of his memoir was scrapped on this basis. At one point, he told Alastair Campbell that he preferred to be out of the UK. He was revered in the United States, among Republicans and Democrats, soon beginning to make a fortune on the speakers' circuit. He had become an unlikely King Lear, not welcome on the terrain he once ruled.

Blair was not especially interested in money, although he liked the high life and enjoyed spending time with the ultra-wealthy. Soon he was part of their world as a figure of considerable affluence as well as being a draw as a glamorous former Prime Minister. What he craved much more was to be close to power, to continue to be relevant as a player. He had been Prime Minister for ten years, had not wanted to stop when he did, and still wanted to be a force across the globe and specifically in the UK. At first the post-Iraq loathing made the UK problematic, and so he toured the world, including negotiating sleeplessly in the Middle East, hoping for a Northern Ireland-style breakthrough. There was not one.

As the years passed, Blair focused more on the UK. He was the first former Prime Minister to establish a huge institute in his name. The Tony Blair Institute (TBI) advised governments across the world. Blair recreated the architecture of his Prime Ministerial life. He had a big town house in London, similar to Number 10, and a large house in the country that had echoes of Chequers. The TBI was the biggest think tank in the UK by a huge margin. Senior staff sent Blair documents that were the equivalent of the red boxes that were part of being a Prime Minister. They erupted with ideas on a range of policy areas, from health reform to Europe. A common link was Blair's passion for the technological revolution. With an even greater intensity he insisted that 'left and right' were irrelevant dividing lines. When accused of lacking an ideological edge he argued somewhat vaguely that the 'centre ground' was values-driven and that it was on this terrain that leaders would make the correct moves. His continued, restless presence on the political scene was unique.

There was no former Prime Minister like him. He continued to command the admiration of a section of the political spectrum ranging from the former Conservative Chancellor George Osborne to those who became Blairites in the Labour Party when he was at his peak. In the media, the columnists who considered themselves to be 'centrists' were as enthusiastic. A lot of senior staff at the BBC also revered him, seeing his politics as being close to theirs, almost a form of impartiality.

Those on the left and right who explored below the surface of his elegant words wondered whether they were as profound as they seemed. With his deep sense of history, Gordon Brown found some of Blair's insights shallow and self-absorbed. The party's former deputy leader, Roy Hattersley, tried to get Blair interested in the writings of R. H. Tawney, but without success. In his final years as Prime Minister his favourite declaration was 'at our best when at our boldest'. Blair liked to see himself as a brave, radical change-maker. But he was a leader who came to power accepting many of the prevailing orthodoxies that had taken hold after 18 years of Conservative rule. He rarely challenged the mighty *Sun* newspaper or powerful business leaders, let alone the United States under Clinton or Bush. Taking on any or all of those mighty forces would take boldness. Blair did not do so.

Yet his three election victories gave him and Brown space to change Britain for the better. The Attlee government was a bigger change-maker, but was out of power after six years. Over ten years, the Blair government secured peace in Northern Ireland, introduced a minimum wage, launched Sure Start, improved the NHS, transformed cities, began the long task of abolishing child poverty, established civil partnerships and imposed a smoking ban. Devolution was implemented fairly smoothly. Free entry to museums and art galleries was reintroduced. The list could go on.

However, whereas the Attlee government established a framework that subsequent Conservative governments did not dare dismantle until after the Thatcher counter-revolution in 1979, the Blair legacy was not so enduring, at least as originally envisaged. Cameron and Osborne destroyed Sure Start with barely a whimper of protest; the Scottish Parliament became for a time the centre of power for an ascendant SNP; Britain left the European Union and in such a manner that the Good Friday Agreement in Northern Ireland became vulnerable. The apolitical language of 'what works is what matters' might have helped Blair stay in power in a country that he assumed leaned to the centre right. But it was not a language that could build a protective edifice around the changes. Without winning an overall majority, Cameron and Osborne pursued new forms of turbo-charged Thatcherism after coming to power in 2010. Soon the sunny optimism of 1997 seemed like distant history. But Blair was far from distant. The most articulate leader in modern times continued to speak out, seeming to make sense of his complex past and at the same time always looking ahead to the hazy future.